GREAT KIDS' ROOMS
COLLECTION

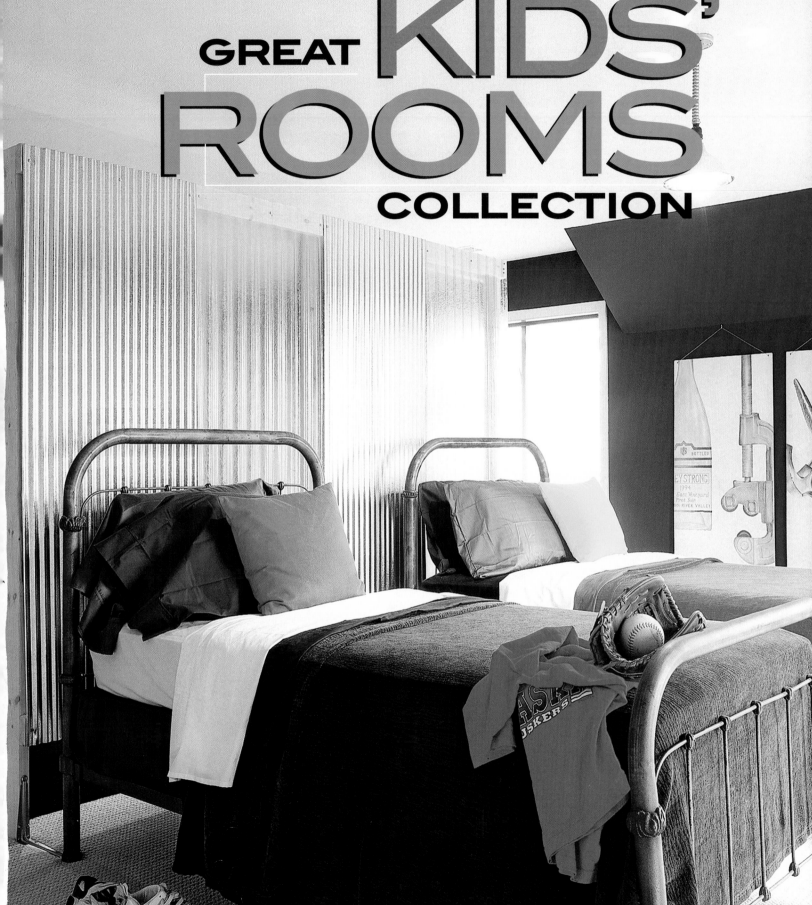

Great Kids' Rooms Collection
Editors: Paula Marshall, Vicki Christian
Contributing Project Manager: Catherine M. Staub, Lexicon Consulting, Inc.
Contributing Editor, Writer: Julie Collins, Lexicon Consulting, Inc.
Contributing Writers: Rachel DeSchepper, Cara Hall, Ellen Kucera,
   Dan Nelson, Missy Peterson, Kelly Roberson, Elizabeth Saunders,
   Lexicon Consulting, Inc.
Contributing Graphic Designer: David Jordan, Studio 22
Copy Chief: Terri Fredrickson
Publishing Operations Manager: Karen Schirm
Senior Editor, Asset & Information Management: Phillip Morgan
Edit and Design Production Coordinator: Mary Lee Gavin
Editorial Assistant: Kaye Chabot
Book Production Managers: Pam Kvitne, Marjorie J. Schenkelberg,
   Rick von Holdt, Mark Weaver
Contributing Copy Editor: Kim Catanzarite
Contributing Proofreaders: Brenna Eldeen, Melinda Garman, Beth Lastine
Contributing Cover Photographer: Gordon Beall
Contributing Indexer: Jana Finnegan

Meredith® Books
Executive Director, Editorial: Gregory H. Kayko
Executive Director, Design: Matt Strelecki
Managing Editor: Amy Tincher-Durik
Senior Editor/Group Manager: Vicki Leigh Ingham
Marketing Product Manager: Steve Rogers

Publisher and Editor in Chief: James D. Blume
Editorial Director: Linda Raglan Cunningham
Executive Director, Marketing: Steve Malone
Executive Director, New Business Development: Todd M. Davis
Executive Director, Sales: Ken Zagor
Director, Operations: George A. Susral
Director, Production: Douglas M. Johnston
Director, Marketing: Amy Nichols
Business Director: Jim Leonard

Vice President and General Manager: Douglas J. Guendel

Meredith Publishing Group
President: Jack Griffin
Executive Vice President: Bob Mate

Meredith Corporation
Chairman and Chief Executive Officer: William T. Kerr
President and Chief Operating Officer: Stephen M. Lacy

In Memoriam: E.T. Meredith III (1933–2003)

All of us at Meredith® Books are dedicated to providing you with information
and ideas to enhance your home. We welcome your comments and suggestions.
Write to us at: Meredith Books, Home Decorating and Design Editorial
Department, 1716 Locust St., Des Moines, IA 50309-3023.

GREAT **KIDS'**
ROOMS
COLLECTION

GREAT KIDS' ROOMS
COLLECTION

Chapter Three:
Teen Retreats

GREAT KIDS' ROOMS COLLECTION

Chapter Five:
Kids' Corner

1 BABY LULLABIES

Chances are your little one sleeps away most of the day, so putting together a nursery that you enjoy as much as he or she does is key. At this point the most important piece of furniture is the place you lay your child's head, so select a crib with care. Then consider what other pieces can grow with your baby, from dressers and wardrobes to toy boxes and bookshelves. Draw inspiration from the wall colors, window treatments, and accessories showcased in this chapter to create a one-of-a-kind nursery that suits your bundle of joy. Select a timeless design and your choices might even take your child from his or her first steps to far beyond that first day of school.

TIMELESS SUITE

A historical home is the fitting location for a nursery suite that sheds the confines of childlike decor and embraces a combination of soft colors, antiques, and art.

Even before they brought their little girl home from the hospital, the homeowners knew they wanted a fun nursery teeming with elegance. They enlisted interior designer Kristi Dinner, who shares their philosophy on decorating for children, to help select furnishings and artwork more sophisticated than the average baby offerings. "There are so many things you can do that are fanciful, fun, whimsical, and childlike without being too cute or juvenile," Dinner says.

Two small rooms connected by a short hallway make up the baby's suite. The rooms themselves—highlighted by beautiful hardwood floors and original moldings—required

IN LIEU OF TYPICAL STORAGE ELEMENTS, AN ANTIQUE CUPBOARD DISPLAYS TOYS AND BOOKS. TWO SMALL PAINTED REPRODUCTION CABINETS FLANK THIS TIMELESS PIECE.

A CLASSIC WOOD CRIB AND MATCHING STORAGE PIECES DEFINE THE SLEEPING QUARTERS. THE CHEST AND OPEN SHELVING HOLD TOYS AND BABY NECESSITIES.

ANTIQUES MIXED WITH NURSERY FURNITURE

TWO-ROOM BABY SUITE WITH NURSERY AND SITTING ROOM

NEUTRAL COLORS AND TIMELESS DECOR

little work besides a fresh coat of paint. Pale yellow walls pair with creamy white trim for a pleasing, neutral backdrop.

In the sitting room, two rocking armchairs sport a fanciful elephant-print fabric and provide a subdued spot for nursing or playing with the baby. Nearby, an antique cupboard stores books and baby memorabilia—as the child grows, she can replace these elements with toys and collectibles. Two painted reproduction cabinets flank the cupboard, offering both storage and style. Framed artwork by Beatle John Lennon lightens up the formal walls. The homeowners purchased the artwork because they thought the whimsical renderings were perfect for a nursery. "I think the highlights of each room are the artwork and antiques," Dinner says. "We really built the room around those pieces."

In the nursery, a classic crib with matching storage pieces create a peaceful haven for baby's sleep. As with most of the elements in the suite, the flower-print rug will be used long after the baby moves into a big-kid bed—further illustrating how timeless pieces trump childlike accessories in this space.

A SHORT HALLWAY CONNECTS THE SITTING ROOM TO THE SLEEPING QUARTERS IN THIS TWO-PART NURSERY. THE EXISTING WINDOWS AND ARCHED DOORWAYS EXUDE HISTORICAL CHARM AND SOPHISTICATION.

ASIDE FROM THE OVERSIZE MADELINE DOLL IN THE SITTING ROOM, THE HOMEOWNERS DID NOT DECORATE WITH RECOGNIZABLE CHILDREN'S CHARACTERS. THIS WAY, THEY BELIEVE, THE TWO ROOMS WILL GROW WITH THE BABY.

The typical baby girl's room might feature pink frills and lacy details, but designer and new mom Jeni Hilpipre-Wright wanted to make baby Maya's room visually distinctive and personally meaningful. Inspired by a trip to the paint store, Wright decided to blend a bold color scheme with children's furniture her grandfather built. An invigorating wall of color gives Maya a room that balances contemporary style with a sense of family history.

INVERTED WOODEN CLOTHES HANGERS SUPPLY AN IMAGINATIVE AND PRACTICAL BANK OF HOOKS.

A VIBRANT WALL OF COLOR DEFINES THIS ROOM. SOFT WHITE ELEMENTS AND FABRICS CREATE A MELLOW HARMONY.

The large blocks of vibrant colors build a stimulating, playful visual space. "I got the idea for the grid wall first," says Wright, who used bold color as a foundation for the entire design. Muted natural green covers an adjacent wall, and the rich blue rug echoes details from the crib's bumper. Featuring a green leaf pattern and a blue-striped border, a sheer apron softens the empty space beneath the crib. The window's curtains coordinate with the apron, repeating the natural design. Shades of red, blue, and orange brighten the furniture and further the sense of a unified space.

Partnering with the room's bright sensibility, clever design keeps the space convenient and attractive for a busy family. Maya's closet boasts a generous shelving system that keeps the room tidy. Industrial-size casters lift the crib to a comfortable height and make room for storage below. Blue pockets on the red upholstered ottoman serve as charming storage pouches that hold favorite playtime things. Inverted wooden coat hangers mounted on a board exemplify the room's creative personality and provide innovative hooks for hats, coats, and clothing.

Wright furnished the room with family keepsakes, thereby establishing a personal dimension. A child-size table, rocking chair, and cabinet the baby's great-grandfather built sport a new finish to match the decor. "Mom had saved the cabinet exactly as we left it as kids," Wright says. "I kept the old latches; they make this sound that brings me right back to my childhood."

FABRIC POCKETS ON THE OTTOMAN'S SLIPCOVER SERVE AS SOFT, PLAYFUL STORAGE FOR STUFFED ANIMALS.

THE CRIB BUMPER FEATURES A FUN DESIGN ON ONE SIDE AND A SOOTHING GREEN TONE ON THE OTHER.

CONTEMPORARY PLAYFULNESS MEETS FAMILY HISTORY IN A REFINISHED CHILD'S PLAY CABINET ORIGINALLY BUILT BY BABY MAYA'S GREAT-GRANDFATHER.

For this designer and mom, the baby's room offers more than a visually inspiring space for a crib. The imaginative combination of personalized design and family treasures creates a truly special room filled with modern vision and a valued past. "It's great to have so much family history in Maya's room," Wright says.

INDUSTRIAL CASTERS ELEVATE THE BED TO A COMFORTABLE LEVEL. A SHEER APRON STYLISHLY COVERS THE STORAGE SPACE BELOW.

SANDED, REPAINTED, AND REUPHOLSTERED, THIS KEEPSAKE ROCKING CHAIR GETS A NEW LOOK AND A NEW LIFE.

ANTICIPATING THE MANY NEEDS OF A NEW BABY, THE BEDROOM CLOSET'S MULTIPLE ORGANIZATIONAL OPTIONS KEEP THE ROOM ORDERLY AND EFFICIENT.

Enduring verses of childhood inspired William Nemer's fairytale bedroom. Humpty-Dumpty sits on a wall above the crib, Mary Quite Contrary tends to her garden, and an enchanted kingdom arises from the lengths of closet doors.

"We started with the idea of wallpaper, but then my husband, Peter, said, 'Let's get someone to paint it across the whole room,'" William's mom, Cindy, says.

The couple worked with decorating artist Susan Robbins, who chose images from nursery-rhyme books, chalking each one on the wall. She then colored them with pastel acrylic paints, the whole of which became a wraparound wonderland.

"I wanted it to feel like you were walking into a storybook," Robbins says. "The design is continuous—the stars from the ceiling come down to the walls, and the trees reach around corners. I chose the 'Star Light, Star Bright' verse to tie it all together, because it's a sleepy bedtime kind of poem."

Not quite 2 years old, William isn't able to read the verse yet, but he often stares spellbound at the wishing stars silhouetted overhead.

"When William gets older, we can use all the images to teach him nursery rhymes," Cindy says. "It's so much better than I ever imagined it could be."

THE MURAL'S COLORS MATCH THE SIMPLE BLUE, WHITE, AND YELLOW PLAID LINENS THAT DECORATE THE CRIB.

BECAUSE THE CLOSET DOORS OPEN AND CLOSE SO OFTEN, ARTIST SUSAN ROBBINS PROTECTED THEM WITH A COAT OF LATEX POLYURETHANE.

Star light, star bright,

A Palace for a Princess

Nestled deep in the American heartland, Asha Leela Hebbar's nursery evokes the splendor of her Indian heritage. "Our real vision was that we could create a room that was a palace for an Indian princess," says her mother, Aviva Ajmera Hebbar. "We incorporated traditional Indian elements, such as the bookshelves, architecture, floor pillows, paisley motifs, and deep saturated colors with splashes of gold. The fabrics really lend authenticity and inspired our design."

To complement the rich feel of the fabric, decorative painter Tina Blanck painted the walls lavender and pink with paisley motifs. A mixture of lilac paint and glaze over a white base created the background for the exotic design.

Blanck then sponged a pink glaze over the areas to receive paisleys, which were then stenciled with gold metallic paint.

The pretty Indian palace will give Asha a sense of her Indian heritage and offer an inspirational retreat where she can reign as princess. "When I walk into the room, I know I'm going into a happy place, an exotic place," Aviva says. "It's my favorite room in the house."

A KALEIDOSCOPE OF FABRICS CREATES THE CUSHION FOR THE WINDOW SEAT, CIRCULAR BOLSTER, AND SQUARE THROW PILLOWS.

PAINTED INDIA-INSPIRED CUTOUTS ABOVE THE BOOKSHELVES REVEAL COLLECTIBLE DOLLS AND STUFFED ANIMALS.

A SIMPLE CANOPY RING AND CURTAINS MADE FROM SHEER PINK FABRIC LEND AN AIRY FEEL TO THIS REGAL SPACE.

Patchwork of fabrics for cushions and pillows

India-inspired cutouts above window seat and shelves

Sheer fabric canopy above crib

BUNNY BLISS

A little bunny named Neuman inspired interior designer Melinda Fitzgerald to create a cuddly blend of babies and bunnies for this room in the Petersburg Symphony Showhouse in Virginia.

The idea for this winning combination originated in a blue-and-white bedding Fitzgerald found, which sports images of the sweet rabbit character. Fitzgerald borrowed the same color combination and used it throughout the nursery. She painted softly striated blue stripes over the previously stark white walls. Then she placed white-painted wooden cutouts of Neuman along the top of the wall as a border and in front of the fireplace. On closer inspection, even more bunny details are evident—the child-size coat rack is topped with a painted bunny, and a soft rabbit-inspired rug covers the hardwood floor.

As with any space tailor-made for a baby, the crib is the centerpiece of the room. A decorative canopy of dotted tulle—which can be moved out of reach for safety—hangs above the crib. The same fabric is repeated on the window to softly filter sunlight.

"This is an 1800s house, and I got the idea [for the canopy] from that time period, when they would leave windows open and protect the baby from pests with netting," Fitzgerald says.

To make the extra-large room even cozier, classic yellow chaise lounges provide spaces for mother and baby to cuddle. Yellow accents round out the soft color scheme.

A DECORATIVE CANOPY OF TULLE OVER THE CRIB SERVES AS A FOCAL POINT. THE BUNNY THEME IS CONSISTENT BUT NOT OVERDONE.

THREE-DIMENSIONAL WOODEN BUNNIES TOP OFF THE STRIATED WALL TREATMENT NEAR THE CEILING.

Anna   Sophie   Maggie

Zachary   Benjamin

Instead of serving as the perfect hiding spot for a game of hide-and-seek, the extra walk-in closet in Beverly and Ray Berry's home provides a cozy nursery for naptime when grandchildren come to play.

Beverly and Ray first contemplated turning the walk-in closet between two guest bedrooms into a sitting area. But designer Linda Knight Carr convinced them to go another route. "I thought; how about a nursery for the grandbabies when they're over at naptime or spending the night," Carr says. "They loved that."

The new nursery is too small to play or gather in, but with its white crib and pine chest it holds everything a baby needs. The top of the chest doubles as a changing table with the simple addition of a pad.

To emphasize the charm of the tiny guest space, Carr papered both the walls and angled ceiling with a petite blue flower print on white paper. The light background visually expands the space, while the floral design keeps it cozy. A paper trim defines the wall from the ceiling, further emphasizing the quirky angles in the room.

The flower-print pattern reappears on the fabric and the window treatment. "The window was either going to be great or a distraction," Carr says. "The shaped awning treatment mimics the wall angles and adds unexpected charm." For light control a matching Roman shade, which is free of hard edges and cords for safety, closes when baby needs to sleep.

Two of the Berrys' five grandchildren were young enough to use the nursery once it was completed. Although they're all too old for the crib now, Beverly says they are not planning to change the space anytime soon. "We've used it a lot with my nieces' and friends' children, and now we have a nice young friend who is expecting, so we're excited to use it again," she says.

FRENCH DOORS LEADING INTO THE NURSERY CAN BE LEFT OPEN TO ALLOW LIGHT IN THE HALLWAY. CLOTH OVER THE PANED DOORS ENSURES THE BABY ENJOYS UNINTERRUPTED SLEEP.

A PILLOW EMBROIDERED WITH THE GRANDKIDS' NAMES DECORATES THE CRIB. THE OTHER PILLOW'S PATTERN MATCHES THE WALLPAPER.

A Dog's Life

It's all about play in this little boy's room that's designed to make the transition from toddlerhood to elementary school easy. "Little boys often grow out of boy-themed rooms quickly," says Amy Barry, who worked with interior designer Linda Knight Carr to design her son Zachary's room. "I wanted to do a boyish theme that was a bit different."

The dog-pattern fabric used on the window seats inspired the room's color scheme. "It's a sophisticated, young fabric," Amy says. "So it won't seem babyish by the time he's in third

A STRIPED WALLPAPER IN NEUTRAL COLORS CREATES A SOPHISTICATED BACKDROP FOR THIS TODDLER'S ROOM.

EMBROIDERED DOGS ADORN THE PLAID WINDOW SEAT FABRIC THAT INSPIRED THE ROOM'S COLOR SCHEME AND DECOR. THE RED FABRIC USED ON THE SIDES OF THE CUSHIONS MATCHES THE VALANCES ABOVE.

THE RED VALANCES INCORPORATE STRIPS OF PLAID-PATTERN CLOTH AND DOG-INSPIRED BLACK, BROWN, AND TAN TASSELS.

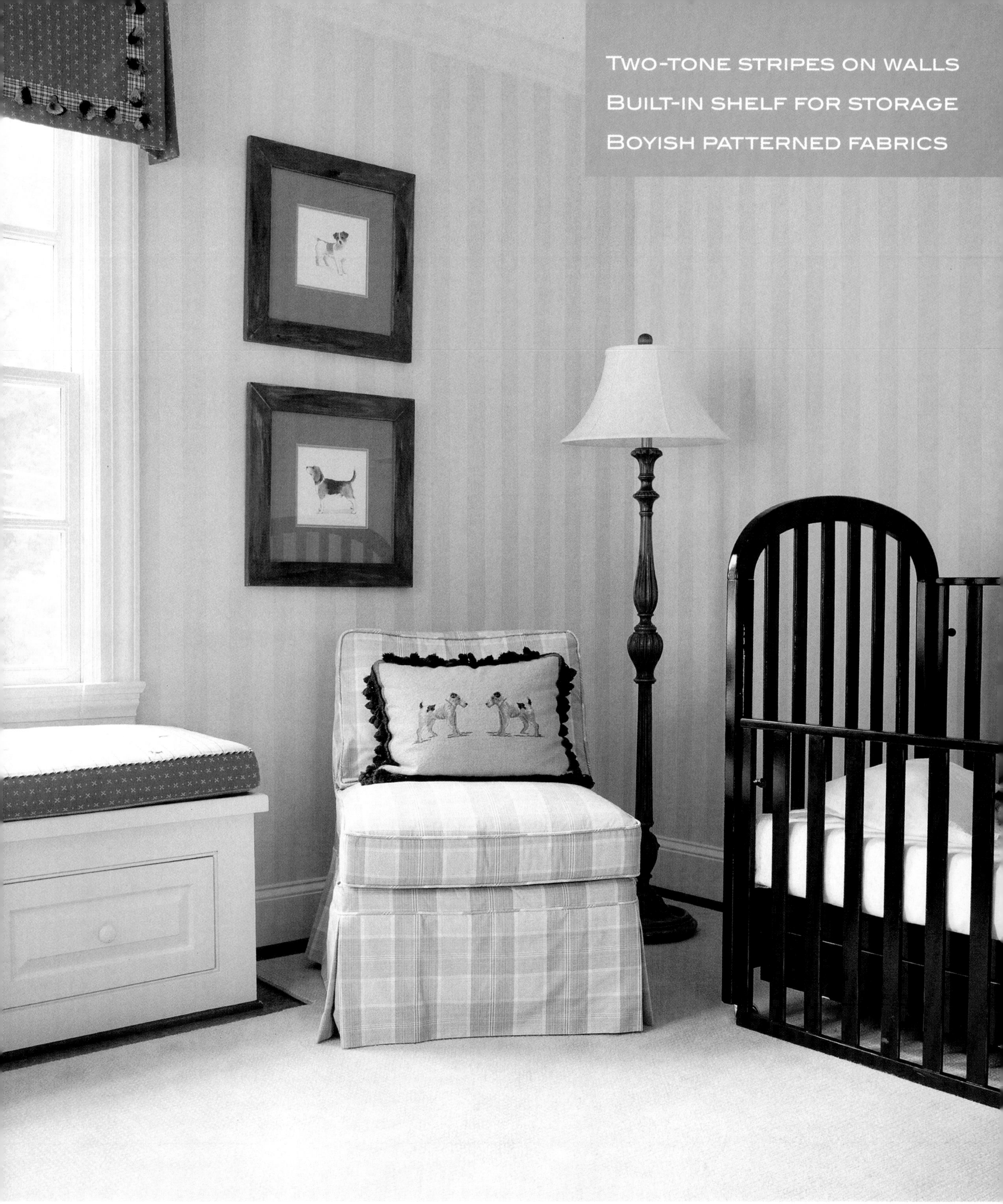

Two-tone stripes on walls
Built-in shelf for storage
Boyish patterned fabrics

BLACK FURNITURE, INCLUDING THIS ANTIQUE
DRESSER, LENDS A MASCULINE TOUCH TO ZACHARY
BARRY'S BEDROOM.

grade." Plaid, stripes, and neutral tones define the space. Wallpaper boasts a taupe-cream two-tone stripe, and a chair is upholstered in a tan plaid fabric. Red and black accents add a masculine touch. The crib and dresser are painted black, while the fabric used on the window treatments and the window seat cushions is a dark red.

Although it's small, Zachary's room seems much larger thanks to built-in furniture. A shelf flanked by window seats provides ample storage for Zachary's toys. "That's what I like about Zachary's room," Amy says. "There's a place to quite literally throw his toys, and they're put away." The upholstered chair, crib, and dresser are the only other pieces of furniture in the room, leaving plenty of floor space for playtime now and in years to come.

MAGNIFICENT MENAGERIE

Beth Keim discovered a fanciful animal rug at her own baby shop, Lucy & Company, and knew right away it was perfect for her baby's nursery. Unsure of whether the child was a boy or a girl, Beth armed herself with the rug and an equally inspiring animal-print sheer for the window, and put together a playful menagerie of animals to greet her forthcoming little one.

Coordinating the nursery's color palette—a scheme of reds, golds, and oranges—with the rest of the house was key for Beth. "I firmly believe each room should flow into the next," she says. "Even if it's a kid's room, I think all the color tones in your whole house ought to be consistent."

The golds in the baby's room meld with similar shades in the hallway and adjacent bedrooms.

RED, GOLD, AND A SPLASH OF BLACK MAKE A STATEMENT IN THIS ANIMAL KINGDOM. THE DAYBED'S PILLOWS COORDINATE WITH THE FABRIC FROM THE VALANCE AND THE CRIB BED SKIRT.

THE GOLD-STRIPED WALLS AND ORANGE POLKA-DOT PILLOWS AND BEDDING ENHANCE THE VIBRANT COLOR PALETTE.

To brighten the space, which originally was a guest room, Beth's husband, Keith, painted two-tone gold stripes on the walls. Beth painted the foot of the daybed to match the valance, and she created the tiger painting that hangs above the bed.

A mix of wood furniture finishes plays off each other in an attractive way. "I tried to use an eclectic mix of furniture because I don't like it all to match," Beth says. The bed is bold red, while the round crib retains its original wood finish. Beth found the black dresser at a flea market and purchased it with intentions of using it elsewhere once the baby outgrows the room.

A big walk-in closet with a changing table means many of the practicalities of a baby's life are hidden from sight, leaving room for more carefully considered details. A slipcovered club chair provides the perfect perch for mother and baby. Beth chose the slipcover for its convenience, as

it's easily removed and washed. Once the baby grows, the chair (like the dresser) can be used elsewhere. The pillows on the bed coordinate with the fabric used on the valance and the crib bedskirt, pulling together all of the enchanting elements in the room.

A SEA GRASS RUG RESTS UNDERNEATH THE INSPIRATIONAL AREA RUG.

ROCKERS AND A SLIPCOVER WERE ADDED TO A BASIC CLUB CHAIR TO CREATE A SPOT FOR ROCKING THE BABY. BETH PAINTED THE ANTIQUE WOODEN TRAIN SET TO MATCH THE ROOM'S COLOR SCHEME.

THE VINTAGE BLACK CHEST, A FLEA MARKET FIND, IS AN ECLECTIC PIECE OF FURNITURE THAT WORKS WELL HERE.

THE PLEATED AND BOWED VALANCE HELPS BRING OUT THE ROOM'S RED AND GOLD COLOR SCHEME.

SERENELY SAGE

A simple, soothing space, this nursery accommodates both parents and child without sacrificing style. Sage and cream stripes set the stage for a peaceful environment. "Sage is an incredibly easy color to live with—it's much more inviting than just plain cream or white," says interior designer Rachel Urban.

A reversible chenille braided rug, soft enough to crawl on, grounds the room's sage and cream striped walls. In front of the tall windows, which are covered with dreamy cotton-organdy panels, sits an iron crib with an antiqued pewter finish. The crib passes today's safety standards, while boasting vintage style. Nearby a down-filled chair covered in a machine-washable slipcover beckons mom or dad to cuddle with baby.

Baby clothes passed down through the generations hang on the wall as historical art.

A BUMPER OF WASHABLE VELVET SOFTENS THE VINTAGE-STYLE CRIB.

PRESSED BETWEEN PANES OF GLASS, BABY CLOTHES FROM FAMILY MEMBERS ADD A PERSONAL TOUCH.

TALL WINDOWS FLOOD THE ROOM WITH LIGHT. A BEADED CHANDELIER CASTS A GENTLE GLOW AT NIGHT.

ORGANDY WINDOW PANELS OF STARCHED COTTON SOFTEN LIGHT WHILE BABY SLEEPS. THEIR BEE DESIGN IS SUBTLE AND SWEET.

VINTAGE-STYLE CRIB WITH VELVET BUMPER

CHANDELIER FOR LIGHTING

SOFT CHENILLE RUG

MIXED, NOT MATCHED

It takes planning—and a little bit of design panache—to pull together fabrics and furniture that don't quite match. But in this one-of-a-kind nursery, Lisa Cook managed to create an elegant, timeless look with her vintage-inspired design. "I like the look of old, put-together stuff," Lisa says. "I just didn't want anything that looks prepackaged or that you could buy at the store."

Lisa began by matching a lighter shade of green paint to a hue she liked in an antique hooked rug. That decision helped tie together the varying fabrics and patterns, including toiles, checks, and stripes in classic shades of deep red, light pink, and tan.

Even though it isn't a matched set, the lines and shapes of the nursery furniture coordinate. Lisa painted a brand-new, antique-looking crib a cream color, sanded the edges for an aged effect, and applied polyurethane for durability. An old armoire, on the other hand, received a fresh coat of rich cream paint, while a new lingerie chest, painted soft green, has sanded edges and crystal drawer knobs for old-fashioned appeal.

Lisa's innate design ability worked its charm on her family. "All three of my daughters used the room when they were babies," she says.

LISA COOK SPRUCED UP THE OLD ARMOIRE WITH A COAT OF PAINT AND REUPHOLSTERED THE COMFY CHAIR WITH NEW FABRIC THAT MIXES THE ROOM'S SOFT PINK WITH MUTED BROWN.

THE NURSERY TAKES ADVANTAGE OF OLD AND NEW PIECES, INCLUDING A NEW LINGERIE CABINET TREATED TO LOOK LIKE AN ANTIQUE.

A LITTLE BIT OF SANDING SOFTENS THE EDGES OF A BRAND-NEW CRIB. FABRIC COLORS ECHO EVERYTHING FROM THE ANTIQUE HOOKED RUG TO THE WALL ACCENTS.

A VARIETY OF ONE-OF-A-KIND FABRICS

CLASSIC GREEN AND CREAM COLOR SCHEME

MIX OF NEW AND ANTIQUE FURNITURE

Strawberry Apple Twist

Little girls and pink go together like chocolate chip cookies and milk. The combination is so delicious, there's no reason to try unsatisfying alternatives. But even the most darling pink rooms need relief from complete saturation.

Designer Ashley Taylor thrives on mixing patterns and colors, so infusing coordinating hues into her baby daughter Libby's room was a delightful challenge. "I wanted to design my daughter's nursery in traditional pinks and greens, but use them in an unexpected way," Ashley says. "So I went on a hunt for some cheerful green gingham. When I found this particular sample, I knew immediately that it would be my overall inspiration for the room. That fabric even inspired me to tear out the carpet and paint the floors gingham!"

Ashley didn't stop with the green gingham—she also introduced hot-pink gingham, a large-scale blue floral, a sheer floral swirl, and plaid silk to the room's repertoire. "Mixing patterns of different scales and textures is a key to creating cozy interiors," she says. "My goal was to find at least five patterns in coordinating colors." Ashley purchased extra yardage of the fabrics, too, so Libby can sleep in coordinated bedding even when she graduates to a twin bed.

The room's accent colors of yellow and blue come from the floral fabric. The whimsical crib, fashioned to look like a four-poster bed, dons a sun-kissed hue paired with fresh white railings and trim. Yellow also makes an appearance on the awning above the window seat and in small decorative touches throughout the space. The color bathes the adjoining bathroom's walls in buttery warmth. Pretty pastel blue brightens the storage baskets within the armoire as well as the toile-covered side chair that rests nearby.

A DAINTY CRYSTAL-CLAD CHANDELIER, CAPPED WITH CUSTOM PINK SHADES, ILLUMINATES FROM HIGH UP.

IN PLACE OF BEIGE CARPETING, THE TAYLORS HAD WIDE-PLANK PINE FLOORING INSTALLED AND PICKLED FOR AN AGED APPEARANCE BEFORE THEY PAINTED THE GINGHAM PATTERN.

CAREFUL DETAILS SUCH AS PLEATED SKIRTS, RICKRACK TRIM, AND GREEN GINGHAM WELTING TIE TOGETHER THE CHAIR AND OTTOMAN'S COLLAGE OF FABRICS.

GINGHAM-PAINTED FLOORING

FABRICS WITH DIFFERENT-SIZE DESIGNS

RIBBON AND OTHER FRILLY ACCENTS

The white crib railing, side table, armoire, and window shutters stand like billowy clouds in a pastel paradise.

"I wanted a look that was bordering on over-the-top, but wasn't too pink or too frilly or too much," Ashley says. "I made sure to go the extra mile to make everything playful and whimsical, while still keeping it super sweet."

A CUSTOM-DESIGNED AWNING HANGS ABOVE THE WINDOW SEAT. ASHLEY TAYLOR USED A GLUE GUN TO ATTACH ARTIFICIAL BLOOMS TO THE AWNING.

EVEN LIBBY'S BUMPER PAD DISPLAYS HER MOM'S AFFINITY FOR MIXING FABRICS AND TRIMS.

THE SUBSTANTIAL ARMOIRE SITS REGALLY IN FRONT OF THE PINK TOILE WALLPAPER. ITS COMBINATION OF OPEN AND CLOSED STORAGE PROVIDES DISPLAY LEDGES AND CLUTTER CONTROL.

TERMS OF ENDEARMENT

Look quickly at a snapshot of the nursery Blis and Chris Freeman created for daughter Lawson, and you might think you're looking at a photo from 1924—the year their Dallas-area home was built. Look closer, however, and you'll notice the sophisticated and stylish details that reveal the room's 21st century origins. "I wanted vintage baby, but I didn't want the room to have a theme," Blis says. She drew inspiration from a well-worn baby book.

Soft and light was the order of the day. Beaded board painted whisper-soft blue lines the walls three-quarters of the way up, and the rest of the room is white. Windows flood the space with light, and soft pastel accents in pink and blue round out the relaxing palette. "I wanted the feeling to be soft and soothing, so I used older toys and antiques," Blis says.

Regular furniture became baby pieces with some modification of their surfaces. An armoire, which once housed a television, received multiple coats of white paint, then some blue diluted with water to accent the scallops and soft pink on the doors. Images copied from an old baby book front the face of the armoire and float on the walls above the beaded board.

True vintage pieces and old-style accents mingle with framed black-and-white photographs of relatives—truly intriguing details for old and young alike. A rosebud-print fabric, sewn inside-out to soften the colors, covers the seat of a new glider rocker. Blis's mom made pillows of varying sizes, all from old flour sack material, and Blis added her childhood oak daybed. "The [nursery] wasn't big enough for a regular bed, but this provides additional seating and a place to lie down with Lawson," Blis says.

Stylish. Nostalgic. Sophisticated. Endearing. Those are terms any girl can grow to love.

Soft cotton scrim provides sheer window coverage. Vintage millinery bouquets bloom at their tops.

The crib's carved details maintain the nursery's soft lines. Wicker baskets under the daybed provide easy access for books, blankets, and toys.

HEIRS

BLIS PAINTED THE BABY'S NAME ON THE CHANGING TABLE, COVERED IT WITH WHITEWASH, AND SANDED IT FOR AN AGED LOOK.

A SPECIAL PAINT TREATMENT USED ON THE DRESSER AND MIRROR PUTS ON NOSTALGIC AIRS.

THE ARMOIRE'S ROSE DRAWER PULLS DECORATE THE SOFTLY PAINTED PIECE WITH SWEET DETAIL.

BABY PINK AND BLUE ACCENTS BEAUTIFY THE ARMOIRE. GENTLE BLUE BEADED BOARD LINES THE WALLS ALMOST TO THE CEILING.

Silken Slumbers

Inspiration comes in many forms and is often found in unexpected places. While helping a client, designer Shannon Jernigan stumbled across an unusual yet irresistible swatch of silk. "I always let fabric drive my choices," she admits. "In this case it was silk polka dots." Little did she know that the unusual swatch would become the basis for a dramatic nursery for her son Cole.

Shannon used the silk's green-and-blue color scheme to build a dreamy, sophisticated space that maintains a touch of childlike whimsy with its polka dots. As the room's lush focal point, Roman shades crown a sun-filled window and provide a broad, defining stage for the silk material. Across the room, a languid sash drapes over three wall pegs, creating a canopy effect around Cole's crib. Although the feature must be altered for safety reasons when Cole is able to reach the material, for the moment it establishes a colorful sense of formality. "I like things dressy," Shannon explains. "Not everyone would be open to using silks in a nursery."

To complement the elegant sensibility, classic details imbue the room with sentimental depth. Sterling silver

LETTERS SPELLING "DREAM" ON THE WALL REFLECT THE ROOM'S SENTIMENTAL MOOD.

A BROAD BAY WINDOW SEAT BALANCES NOSTALGIC COMFORT WITH CLASSIC ELEGANCE.

keepsakes, black-and-white photography, and family mementos promote a pleasing heirloom quality. A spacious window seat and classic detailing on the room's fixtures evoke a nostalgic impression of bygone Victorian splendor. "The vintage feel gives detail and character to the room," Shannon says.

The decor exudes a distinctive refinement, but the room remains a practical nursery. A soft gliding rocker eases late-night comforting sessions, and a thick backing on the silken shades ensures darkness on sunny days. "I lined the shades with blackout lining for sleepy mornings and to create a good nap environment," Shannon says.

The room's design also accommodates the changing demands of a maturing child. Bookshelves and generous

Lush silk drapes and an inviting rocker make the nursery an attractive destination for parents too.

Rich classic elements coordinate with the more whimsical features of childhood, such as this teddy bear, for an overall sophisticated nursery.

drawers hold a growing collection of books and toys, while an open floor area permits active play without disrupting the room's decorative elements. Once the baby outgrows the elegant iron rail crib, it transforms easily into a daybed suitable for years to come.

Personalized details ensure the space is a comforting, dreamy refuge for the parents as well as the child. A traditional family nighttime prayer—"God bless the moon and God bless me"—is painted above the grand window. While the verse connects the family to its past, it also establishes the room's mood. Painted on the walls or hanging from the ceiling, moons and stars lend a contemplative, universal feel to the decor. "I wanted a spiritual feel to the room," Shannon says. "After all, a child is a gift from God."

DRAPED OVER THREE WALL PEGS ABOVE THE CRIB, THE ROOM'S DEFINING POLKA-DOT SILK FABRIC MIMICS THE FORMAL APPEARANCE OF A CANOPY.

A MOBILE ABOVE THE CRIB PLAYFULLY REFLECTS THE ROOM'S HEAVENLY THEME.

Color Me Cute

What's a baby to do? Little Ella needed to hit the ground running, so to speak, if she was to keep up with two trendy big sisters. So her parents knew a traditional sugar-and-spice nursery, with pretty ruffles and little bows, wouldn't cut it.

"We wanted her nursery to be bright and fun like her sisters' rooms," says designer Kim Dwyer. "A babyish nursery just wouldn't have been a good fit for this family. We assured the parents, 'You don't have to use pastel pinks and blues in a baby's room.'" Dwyer considered the other girls' rooms, boldly decked out in turquoise and purple, before deciding on the equally strong tones of hot pink, orange, and red for Ella's room.

Dwyer selected a patterned rug with several shades of pink and orange to serve as the room's focal point. The rug provided inspiration for nearly every design decision that followed. "With such great shades of pink in that rug, we decided to do two variations of those shades on the walls in big horizontal stripes," she notes. "The stripes made a bold statement and also help the room appear larger." Referring again to the rug, Dwyer selected orange with pink fabrics for the curtains and to dress up the dark wooden crib. Polka dots and squiggles abound.

The furniture also displays bold details. Dwyer handpainted orange bands around the dresser drawers and polka dots on the dresser top.

"No fear" is her biggest piece of advice for parents-to-be. "A lot of people just aren't used to seeing nurseries in vivid colors. But if you pick colors your child is still going to like in a few years, you won't be sorry."

HANDPAINTED WALLS IN BRILLIANT RASPBERRY AND PEONY PINK SURROUND THE CRIB. WHIMSICAL CHARACTERS FLOAT ABOVE.

DESIGNER KIM DWYER HANDPAINTED CHEERFUL DOTS ON THE DRESSER TOP TO MATCH THE UPHOLSTERED ROCKER AND PILLOWS.

TANTALIZING FABRICS MIX AND MATCH ON THE WINDOW SEAT.

A VINTAGE WHITE-PAINTED MIRROR AND DRESSER
STAND OUT AGAINST THE BROAD WALL STRIPES.
ORANGE BANDS FRAME THE DRAWERS.

SUNLIGHT WARMS A COZY WINDOW SEAT FILLED WITH
FLUFFY PATTERNED PILLOWS.

THE ROOM'S JAZZY CELEBRATION OF COLOR AND
PATTERN INCLUDES AN ORANGE LAYERED LAMP,
POLKA-DOT UPHOLSTERY, AND SQUIGGLY PATTERNED
CURTAINS.

MOD SQUAD

Contemporary taste needn't be banished from a baby's room. When Diane Ashbee and her husband Richard found out they were having their first child, they took the same approach to decorating the nursery as they had taken in the rest of the home.

"We live in a high-rise, and the rest of our apartment has lots of contemporary java tones," Diane says. "So

MODERN TAN, BROWN, BLUE, AND GREEN HUES

BASIC POLKA-DOT PATTERNS

FURNITURE THAT "GROWS" WITH THE BABY

LETTERS PAINTED TO MATCH THE ROOM'S FABRICS SPELL THE LITTLE OCCUPANT'S NAME. LANDON LIKES TO POINT AT THE LETTERS AND SAY EACH ONE.

THIS ANGELA ADAMS RUG HAS DOODLES THAT FORM RIDGES IDEAL FOR DRIVING TOY CARS.

it didn't seem right to have one room be all ducks and bears and pastels. But, at the same time, I wanted it to be welcoming."

Diane collaborated with interior designer Joani Stewart to create the playful, pretty room where robin's-egg blue walls pair with crisp white trim. "It's not your typical baby blue, but it's a nice soft, calming color," Diane says. "Like the rest of the room, it has a depth that can grow with him."

A playful Angela Adams rug adorns the floor. Its swirls lend the feeling of movement, while its blue, green, and chocolate colors unite the room's color scheme. Clean-lined furniture balances out the vibrant pattern. "You don't want to overwhelm a room with pattern," Stewart says.

The deep brown, or java, colored crib, side tables, and changing table shelving unit impart a sophisticated, contemporary feel. A khaki slipcovered rocking chair entices cuddling before bedtime.

Careful furniture selection ensures that the room will age gracefully. The crib features a gently arching back and slightly fluted legs. When Landon outgrows the crib railings, the piece will convert to a full-size bed. With the removal of the changing pad, a classy changing table becomes a large bureau and bookcase. The side tables that house toys now can flank Landon's bed as night tables when he graduates from his crib.

A fitting partner to the sophisticated nursery, Landon's bathroom boasts stylish form with pragmatic touches. Apple-green glass tiles covering the walls and countertops play contrast with the cabinetry and mirror frame, which feature a dramatic java finish. "We wanted to keep the look chic," Stewart says, "but we moved the sink off to one side to make way for a baby bathtub and added a single-handle faucet to make it easier for Landon to operate." Curved white pendent lamps take a modern approach to vanity lighting.

Through the thoughtful selection of colors and patterns, and the integration of helpful details, the nursery suits Landon and seamlessly integrates with the rest of the home. "It's a kid's room with style," Stewart says. "It has an understated elegance to it, yet it's still child-friendly because of all the whimsical touches."

SPARKLY APPLE-GREEN GLASS TILES LIGHTEN UP THE BATHROOM AND ENTICE A TOUCH OF PLAYFULNESS.

DIAPERS AND CLOTHES STAY OUT OF SIGHT BUT CLOSE AT HAND IN DRAWERS BENEATH THE BABY CHANGING STATION.

BLUE SKY BABY

Little Graham Josephson begins and ends each day with nothing but blue sky, thanks to his parents David and Tara. They hired designer Terri Ervin to create this Beatrix Potter-themed nursery for the new little Josephson.

The room's heavenly ceiling continues partway down the wall, producing a more realistic effect. It's a fine backdrop for the fanciful bunnies, birds, and mice that share the room.

Cheerful yellow shines brightly in Graham's storybook nursery. The cottage-style crib, with its white picket headboard, footboard, and garden-theme finials, serves as a focal point for the room. At the windows, dotted sheers with yellow-and-white stripe banding keep the look whispy and light.

Although blue plays a prominent role, the nursery is designed to serve children of either gender. "It would work as well for a girl as it does a boy," Ervin says. "Tara could simply play up the greens and yellows, instead of the blues."

Graham's parents love their son's nursery. "We were really looking for something fun, and we love it," Tara says. "It's the cutest thing."

A CRISSCROSS PATTERN OF WHITE RIBBON HOLDS PHOTOS AND OTHER BABY MEMENTOS IN PLACE AGAINST A YELLOW FABRIC-COVERED DISPLAY BOARD.

SUNSHINE-YELLOW FURNISHINGS AND ACCENTS STAND OUT AGAINST THE BLUE CEILING AND WALLS IN GRAHAM JOSEPHSON'S STORYBOOK NURSERY.

WHITE PICKETS ON THE CRIB
BLUE SKY PAINTED ACROSS CEILING
SUNSHINE-YELLOW ACCENTS

CHILDLIKE DREAMS

In the years that pass between first words and the first day of middle school, a child's days and nights are filled with imaginative dreams only youth can muster. Decorate your child's room with his or her favorite colors and belongings, and sweet dreams are sure to follow. Start with the necessities: A bed that beckons each night, floor space for imaginative play, and ample storage for clothes and toys. Go all out with wall colors and bedding your kids love—such elements infuse a room with personality and are easy to change as tastes do. Whether your little girl adores pastels or your son wants a room crowded with his favorite storybook characters, you'll find this chapter chock-full of bedrooms that both kids and parents are sure to love.

BUG TIME

Critters have overtaken this little boy's bedroom—and you can't blame them. When interior designer Karen Osborne created this creepy-crawly bedroom for the Koch Model Homes showhouse, she imagined the inhabitant of this room to be an elementary-age boy who loved everything outdoors.

Playing off the windows' wooded view, Osborne chose to paint three walls a warm golden yellow embellished with a tree mural. Colorful bedding covered in bugs, frogs, and leaves inspired the room's various artwork. The old saying "Don't let the bedbugs bite" is stenciled above the bed, and three larger-than-life bugs (borrowed from the pillow shams) reside on canvases hung on the green wall above the dresser. Even the window treatments further the outdoorsy theme—Osborne selected colors and materials reminiscent of a tent for the curtains and valances.

A local craftsman built the hand-hewn headboard and nightstand from massive pieces of wood. The sturdy furniture, including a handsome dresser large enough to accommodate a growing boy's wardrobe, was selected with durability and longevity in mind.

Osborne continued the animal infestation in the bathroom, but because the imagined little boy shares the space with

THE CUSTOM-DESIGNED GOLD, GREEN, AND RED WINDOW TREATMENT IS REMINISCENT OF A TENT PITCHED IN THE WOODS.

SUNLIGHT ILLUMINATES YELLOW WALLS, MAKING A WARM CLIMATE SUITED TO BUGS, FROGS, AND TURTLES.

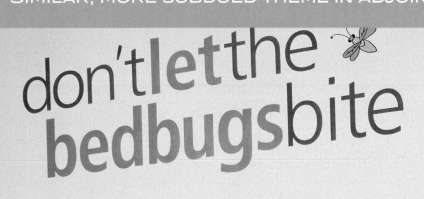

don't let the
bedbugs bite

his sister, the bathroom bugs are more subdued. Butterflies fly, grasshoppers leap, and caterpillars creep across the wallpaper and its leafy border. The multicolor bands along the bottom of the shower curtain pick up the colors of the bugs in the wallpaper. Most important, both bed and bath are tastefully decorated and at the same time playful rooms.

DARK GREEN PAINT ACCENTS THE DRESSER WALL, A BACKDROP FOR THREE BUGS ON CANVAS.

THIS IMAGINATIVE BEDDING INSPIRED A BUG-THEME BEDROOM PERFECT FOR A LITTLE BOY WHO LOVES THE OUTDOORS. A LOCAL CRAFTSMAN FASHIONED THE RUSTIC HEADBOARD AND NIGHTSTAND.

A BUZZING BEE DRAWS ATTENTION TO THE SAYING ON THE HEADBOARD WALL.

The colors in the shower curtain echo those found in the leafy border growing 10 inches below the bathroom ceiling.

The use of butterflies and cheerful colors ensures a happy insect experience.

PRETTY IN PINK

For a little girl who loves to play princess, reigning over this colorful kingdom is a dream come true.

The "Princess Annie" banner mother Lila Niswanger purchased for her daughter inspired interior designer Cortney Singleton to pair a color palette of pinks and greens with polka dots and stripes. Such a design fulfills Annie's wish and will last long after she outgrows the princess theme.

The spacious room boasts a bay window that overlooks the backyard. Singleton used it as the focal point for the room and the backdrop for the bed. "It really is a princess kind of room," Singleton says. "There's that big bay window and high ceilings, so we wanted to exaggerate that as much as possible while keeping the room fun and young."

Princess Annie

A

By selecting hot pink and green, as well as a lighter accent shade in each color, Singleton ensures the color scheme will work for a teen as well as it does for a child. "The softer you go with colors the more 'Barbie' they look, so to grow it up we used hot pinks and dark greens," Singleton says.

The color scheme is particularly evident in the window treatment, which combines blinds, pink sheers, and thick polka-dot-print drapes with blackout lining. The "Princess Annie" banner hangs in front of the windows and above a white-painted bed with custom bedding covered in ruffles, cording, and button details. "The pink sheers and bedding fit the princess theme," Singleton says. "And as Annie gets older, some of the pink accents can be changed to green for an entirely different look."

Fun, frilly details complement the royal color treatment. Green-painted wire side tables topped with fanciful lamps flank the bed, and a pink-painted chandelier goes girly with fabric- and fur-trimmed shades. Along a nearby wall, a child-size sitting area with chairs, a toy chest, and a rack for hanging dress-up accessories is the perfect spot for a princess to primp.

Of course, the best gauge of a bedroom's success is how well its inhabitant reacts to it. Singleton says Princess Annie went "absolutely wild" when she saw her completed bedroom—a sure sign that this royal room made the grade.

Designer Cortney Singleton selected green bedside tables to match the color scheme. The lamp's crystal-like base and rosy white shade balance the abundance of color in the room.

This simple white dresser stands out against the green walls. Ceramic flower knobs get the attention they deserve on this simple piece of painted furniture.

Sheet metal inserts ensure little belongings stay in place on the bedside tables.

THE GREEN QUEEN

A child's likes and dislikes may persevere clear into adulthood, but chances are her tastes will change many times before she reaches her teenage years. With this in mind, homeowner Amy Barry consulted with her daughter Sophie Rose and interior designer Linda Knight Carr to create a timeless bedroom both mother and daughter could love for years to come.

"Even at the age of four, Sophie knew she wanted a green room," Amy says. "Sophie's room reflects her personality—she's very spunky and really lights up a room, but she's also a homebody who loves toys and stuffed animals." To accommodate both sides of Sophie's personality, a whimsical combination of green stripes and plaids dominates the room, while plenty of functional storage options corral belongings.

A SINGLE PAINTING HANGS ABOVE A TRUNDLE BED IN SOPHIE'S BEDROOM. THE ENTIRE SPACE—INCLUDING THE WALLS, BEDDING, AND NIGHTSTAND—ARE AWASH IN SHADES OF GREEN.

THE GREEN AND PINK COLOR SCHEME TOOK CUES FROM A GREEN AND CREAM CHECK CHAIR AND

OTTOMAN THE HOMEOWNERS ALREADY HAD. NEARBY A PAINTED ANTIQUE BOOKSHELF HOUSES STUFFED ANIMALS AND CHILDHOOD MEMORABILIA.

THE CREAM-COLOR ARMOIRE AND A WINDOW SEAT WITH GREEN-PATTERNED CUSHION STORE TOYS, BOOKS, AND OTHER BELONGINGS.

Thanks to the green-papered wall, the eye is drawn to the cream-color trundle bed, which boasts a green-and-white stripe bedskirt and plenty of patterned pillows. "Sophie loves her bed. She already said she's going to pass it on to her favorite child," Amy says.

Across from the bed, a built-in armoire flanked by cushioned window seats stores books, games, and clothing.

Numerous windows framed by draperies and custom-designed beaded valances allow light to enter during the day. At night an antique chandelier lends a soft glow.

"The fabrics and the color schemes are something that are a bit timeless, that Sophie could certainly grow with," Amy says. "Her room suits her personality well."

A green-painted antique metal table serves as a charming nightstand.

As she grows, Sophie may choose to replace her childhood collectibles with more grown-up memorabilia.

The playful valances feature green and white stripes and colorful wooden beads.

WATER WORLD

Octopus, sea horse, and fish friends surround Collin Hanson in his aquariumlike room. Dad Todd took just two days to create the grinning, googly-eyed denizens of the deep after pulling inspiration from a snorkeling trip with his wife, Barb, and Dr. Seuss stories he enjoyed as a child.

To separate sea from sky, Todd painted the top half of the walls light blue and the lower half a deeper shade. Using books and a fish-identification map as guides, he painted tropical-color creatures on the wall and outlined the creatures with thick and thin strokes to make the images "pop." He carefully arranged the sea creatures and clumps of coral so Collin can easily view and enjoy them.

The blue and white bedding on Collin's bed complements the sea scene, and gauzy white curtains provide privacy while creating an under-the-sea glow. To complete the underwater world, stuffed animals hang from invisible strands of fishing line and float freely around the room.

"I put the octopus and the turtle peeking up on either side of the changing table, so Collin could see them when he was lying there," Todd says. "I lined up yellow fish where he could see them through the slats on his crib. The first time we took him in and pointed to things, he oohed and aahed."

DR. SEUSS-INSPIRED WORDS APPEAR HERE, THERE, AND EVERYWHERE ON THE WALLS. A FIBERBOARD CORNICE TOPS THE BREEZY SHADES, MIRRORING THE SHAPE OF THE WALL'S WAVES.

PAYING CAREFUL ATTENTION TO DETAIL, TODD HANSON OUTLINED THE SEA CREATURES WITH BLACK PAINT AND ADDED SHADOW SO THEY'RE ALMOST THREE-DIMENSIONAL.

Big Angles, Little Angel

Rather than try to camouflage the sharply angled walls of this little girl's room in the Boston Junior League Designer Showhouse, designer Kate Dickerson decided to "go with it and use a really bold wallpaper to envelop the whole room," she says. People often think a strong pattern will make an angular room too claustrophobic, but Dickerson disagrees. "They see a slanted ceiling and don't know what to do," she says. "I think it works great with a lot of pattern."

Dickerson chose a bold pink-on-green toile wallpaper for its potential longevity. The color scheme will appeal to a little girl, and the print is one she can grow up with. Childlike accents such as the rocking horse, toy box, and stuffed animals win a little girl's heart. When that same little girl becomes a teen, it will be easy to remove the girlish details and replace them with color appropriate pillows and a few accents without disrupting the room's overall design.

THIS BOLD TOILE WALLPAPER WILL WORK WHEN SHE'S A LITTLE GIRL AND WHEN SHE'S A TEEN.

A SWEET PINK-AND-WHITE CHECK SILK ORGANZA VALANCE WITH CRYSTAL-BEAD TRIM HANGS OVER A COZY WINDOW SEAT PERFECT FOR DAYDREAMING.

LARGE-PATTERNED WALLPAPER
SILK WINDOW TREATMENTS
COZY WINDOW SEAT NOOK

Butterfly Garden

When designer Jeni Hilpipre-Wright took on sprightly Alyson Leusink's new bedroom, Wright knew the 3-year-old's sunny disposition deserved a sunny personal retreat. Soothing pastels, flowered fabrics, and butterflies dangling from the ceiling make up Alyson's own enchanted garden.

Wright handmade the fabric and tissue butterflies that flutter throughout the room. "I thought butterflies flying around the room would add dimension and be interactive for Alyson," Wright says. Like small hanging sculptures, the butterflies add dashes of color and serve as an intriguing kinetic element. "The butterflies are so pretty," says Alyson's mother, Angela. "I really love the way Alyson reacts to them. When the heat or air comes on in her room, the butterflies gently sway."

And where there are butterflies, there are flowers. Delicate floral patterns decorate the bedspread and the sheer fabric of the breezy, ruffled bedskirt. To mute the silver bed frame's reflective quality, the skirt material covers the headboard and footboard. "It is almost like we slipcovered the entire bed," Wright says. "I wanted the look uninterrupted."

Wright chose a glowing background of pastel tones to enhance the room's warm, natural presentation. Pink walls and a sunny yellow set of drawers complement the touches of blue and green in the area rug. Playful butterflies scatter about the pink walls. Above the dresser, doll clothes mounted on colored paper and displayed in six shadow boxes line up for an interesting visual display.

Visually rich and imaginative, this room's character draws as much from Alyson's efforts as from her personality. In order to build a personal connection, Wright involved the young girl in the room's creation: Alyson helped hang the floating butterflies and wall-stamped a few of their counterparts. "Alyson did some stamping and she was very proud of that," Wright says. "I wanted the space to be feminine and fun, just like her."

LIVE FLOWERS NATURALLY ENHANCE THIS GARDEN-INSPIRED BEDROOM.

EASILY AND INEXPENSIVELY CONSTRUCTED, FABRIC AND TISSUE BUTTERFLIES ESTABLISH A PLAYFUL MOOD.

THE BEDDING'S FLOWER PATTERNS COORDINATE WITH THE ROOM'S BRIGHT TONES.

FABRIC AND TISSUE BUTTERFLIES HANGING FROM CEILING

SHEER SLIPCOVERS MUTE THE BRIGHT, METALLIC TONES

DOLL CLOTHES MOUNTED IN SHADOW BOXES

FRAMED DOLL CLOTHING ARTISTICALLY EXPRESSES
ALYSON'S INNER FASHION DESIGNER.

THE COLORFUL BUTTERFLY THEME CONTINUES ON
THE BED, WHERE A BLUE GINGHAM PILLOW IS SHAPED
LIKE ONE.

A SHEER FABRIC DOTTED WITH EMBROIDERED
FLOWERS COVERS THE HEADBOARD AND FOOT-
BOARD, LENDING A ROMANTIC AIR.

Decorative paint store owner Patricia Orlando has every fancy paint finish at her fingertips. But when it came to son Christopher's bedroom, she wanted an easy-to-execute look he could enjoy at the height of his bulldozer and cherry-picker mania.

"The primary colors we used in his room are, to me, boy colors," Patricia says. She painted the chests and table with her own line of highly pigmented furniture paint, then coordinated the room using the same paint for a construction-site wall mural inspired by Christopher's books and toys. Patricia penciled in the pictures, color-washed the background and "road" with one-step yellow and blue glazes, and finished the pictures with latex paint outlined with black paint pen.

Unable to find children's bedding she liked, Patricia sewed bedding from adult sheets in plaid percale and red jersey. The twin duvet cover is edged in a twisted cording that also edges the red throw pillows.

Christopher contributed to the room decor with finger-painted pictures in primary colors. The nicely arranged and framed artwork helps tie together the dresser corner. He can create more drawings on a worktable coated with chalkboard spray paint.

The red dresser sports a stencil of a road crew worker applied at a toddler's eye level. To coordinate, the blue dresser has a fabric insert made from extra plaid sheeting, which Patricia stapled to the back of the removable door panel. The result is a brightly colored work and play site for a future foreman.

COLORFUL DETAILS, INCLUDING A ROAD WORKER PAINTED AT A TODDLER'S EYE LEVEL AND PLAID SHEETING, COORDINATE THE TWO DRESSERS.

CHALKBOARD PAINT TRANSFORMS AN ORDINARY KIDS' TABLE INTO A FUN DRAWING SURFACE.

BOOKS AND TOYS INSPIRED THE HANDPAINTED CONSTRUCTION-SITE WALL MURAL.

Two different girls, two different tastes. Tara Josephson's 11-year-old daughter Abby loves the hippie look. Eight-year-old sister Molly partakes in her mother's passion for purple. One thing the two sisters shared was a bedroom and play space in need of an update. To create a room that enticed the two, Tara turned to interior designer Terri Ervin, who matched inventive colors with perky accents in an irresistible preteen scheme. "Instead of the bead thing, we went with the big, funky flowers," Tara says.

A practical, multicolor, ready-made quilt, with its purple, green, and yellow squares, provided the room's palette. Ervin customized the quilt with a plaid dust ruffle and dressed up the ready-made shams with polka-dot fabric ruffles. "I like to use more affordable comforters for kids' rooms," Ervin says. "It doesn't make sense to spend a lot of money on the thing the kids are going to jump on."

The plaid and polka dots reappear on an awning hung over the playroom door and as tiebacks on the window treatments. Whimsical flowers sprout from boxes under framed mirror "windows" and at the tops of curtain panels.

Though Ervin tempered the purple with a lime green, and the '60s "flower power" anthems received a 21st-century update, Abby and Molly have no complaints. "When the girls first saw the finished room, they thought it was magical," Tara says. "It's such a fun room. Those flowers are just so groovy."

DRESSED IN A PLAID SKIRT, A VANITY STOOL PARKS IN FRONT OF A MIRROR AND WINDOW BOX. A PLAID AWNING ANNOUNCES THE ENTRANCE TO THE PLAYROOM.

FLOWERS BLOOM ON THE BED'S HEADBOARD AND FOOTBOARD, ON THE LAMPSHADE, AND ABOVE THE CURTAIN PANELS. GIANT DRAGONFLIES HOLD BACK THE CURTAINS.

HAPPY TRAILS

Little wranglers need plenty of room to roam free—and lots of storage to corral their gear. A Western-theme bedroom with a custom loft for a focal point skillfully ropes the bullish task.

The substantial-size loft, made with standard lumberyard supplies, has sturdy ladder rungs and guardrails for when the cowboy needs a little shut-eye. A built-in bench and shelving unit camp out under the bed, joined by a movable chair and table. This sets the scene for adventure and excitement and maximizes the open floor space for play. The room abounds in cowboy detail: A horseshoe lamp, leather fringe shelf decoration, and a rug that resembles leafy ground all enhance the Wild West charm.

On another side of the ranch, a barn-shape armoire stows blankets and other supplies. Built-in shelves surround a window, mingling books and toys with decorative items. A mobile game table, fitted with a Western scene and train track, increases the versatility of the space.

A STAR BORDER BRINGS TO MIND SHERIFFS AND THEIR DEPUTIES. THE COTTON ROMAN SHADES SPORT A BARBED-WIRE PATTERN.

COWBOY SCENES ON 1940S-STYLE BARK CLOTH OUTFIT THE WINDOW PANELS AND A PONY-SIZE CLUB CHAIR.

DECORATIVE PAINTING, A HORSE STATUE, WOVEN BLANKETS, AND COILED ROPE BRING THE WILD WEST INTO THIS BEDROOM.

Custom-made loft bunkhouse

Movable Western-theme game table

Barn-shape painted armoire

GARDEN WHIMSY

A tangy trio of watermelon pink, lime green, and lemon yellow brings out the glow in this garden party bedroom.

"I think bright is exciting; it's vibrant. It gets you pumped," says Karen Diggins of her daughter's room. "I think the colors, as vibrant as they can be, are also soft by nature. It's a very soothing room, even though it has a lot of strong color."

A fanciful pink fabric with images of flowers, watering cans, and bugs supplied the inspiration for the wall's handpainted images. "It doesn't have that stenciled look—which makes it fun," says interior designer Michelle

Doughtie. "Every flower is different since it was painted freehand."

A traditional valance, drapery, and a princess canopy for the queen-size bed ground the spirited room in a touch of formality. The bed's white matelassé cover, white rocker, and white wicker dresser and mirror tone down the vibrant colors and patterns.

Kiwi-color terry cloth fabric puts a fanciful twist on a swivel club chair. The white wicker dresser furthers the room's garden party theme.

Hot pink plaid saturates this small bathroom space adjoining the bedroom.

CANOPY ON WALL BEHIND BED
TERRY CLOTH-COVERED SWIVEL CLUB CHAIR
QUEEN-SIZE BED AND CRIB IN SAME ROOM

THIS ROOM WAS DESIGNED WITH A CRIB AND A QUEEN-SIZE BED, SO IT'S READY TO GROW WITH THE CHILD.

THE DESIGNS ALONG THE WALL WERE FIRST DRAWN AND THEN PAINTED USING FINE-TIPPED ARTIST BRUSHES. LATEX EGGSHELL PAINTS ASSURE A WASHABLE FINISH.

Nostalgic Adventure

Bold primary colors typically inhabit children's worlds, but when Kelly Rawlings and her husband Mark Hillenbrand set out to remodel the bedroom of their son, Grant, they didn't even consider bright hues. "I'd had enough of those with Legos," Kelly says.

Instead she wanted the room to reflect the colors of a simpler era. "I'm very fond of things from the 1940s because of the classic, nostalgic look," she says. "So for some time, I had been collecting very innocent and sweet calendar prints of boys and dogs."

The warm, faded hues of the 1940s calendar prints—which Kelly found at antiques stores and online auctions—were exactly what she had in mind. The goal was to create a timeless space that would nurture Grant's love of adventure, exploration, and fun. "I wanted to decorate just once," Kelly says, "and have the room grow with him."

Kelly and Mark enlisted the help of designer David Anger to bring about the comfortable, imaginative atmosphere they envisioned, as well as to find storage space beyond the one small closet in the 9½×10-foot bedroom. He used simple solutions to transform the tiny space into a world of imaginative play, cozy comforts, and plenty of storage.

A snug Pullman car-style bed occupies an entire window wall of the room. The sturdy structure of ¾-inch plywood has an arched opening that forms an alcove for the bed. The face of the bed is painted moss green. Its interior shelves complement the vintage hue with rich terra-cotta that matches the framed prints on the walls.

"The bed is like a tiny room within a room," Anger says. "Kids love to be transported, and this bed does that by becoming everything from a train car to a little theater."

THE RESILIENT CORK FLOOR WITHSTANDS DAMAGE FROM DROPPED TOYS.

BUILT-IN STORAGE DRAWERS BELOW THE BED STOW GRANT'S SMALLER PLAYTHINGS, SUCH AS GAMES AND TOYS.

THE BUILT-IN BED, FRAMED BY AN ARCHED CUTOUT, RESEMBLES THE SLEEPING QUARTERS OF A TRAIN AND SETS THE STAGE FOR SLEEP, PLAY, AND STORAGE. ROMAN SHADES WITH A MAP-PRINT FABRIC COVER THE WINDOWS.

VINTAGE CALENDAR PRINTS INSPIRE COLOR PALETTE

PULLMAN CAR-STYLE BUILT-IN BED

MAPS DECOUPAGED TO DRESSER DRAWERS

Drawers tucked into the base of the unit are perfect for stowing games, toys, and puzzles. Nearby vertical cabinets hold larger items, such as baseball bats, and also make great hide-and-seek spaces for Grant. Terra-cotta-color shelves at the head and foot of the bed are ideal for favorite books, stuffed animals, and knickknacks.

The nostalgic theme takes to the sky with antique biplanes zooming through the wallcovering's clouds. Anger helps plant the seeds for exploration by using map-print fabric bordered in a vintage-brown plaid for Roman shades. The map motif repeats on the dresser—Kelly covered the drawers in color copies made from the pages of a world atlas and painted the rest of the piece a rich golden color.

To finish the room, Kelly and Mark chose cork flooring. "We wanted warmth and comfort," Kelly says. "We did the research and found out that cork is a little bit more resilient than laminate or wood and tends to be warmer. It is so resilient that if Grant drops one of his big Tonka trucks on it, no mark should show."

Grant spends plenty of time in his brand-new vintage haven. Not only does he sleep well in his built-in bed, he often cozies up with the big bolsters to read. The space serves as everything from a stage to a boat to a secret hideout, fueling his of love of adventure and fun.

TERRA-COTTA-COLOR SHELVES AT THE HEAD AND FOOT OF THE BED KEEP BOOKS, STUFFED ANIMALS, AND A FEW KNICKKNACKS CLOSE AT HAND.

THE 1940S CALENDAR PRINTS KELLY RAWLINGS FOUND INSPIRED THE VINTAGE LOOK AND COLORS FOR GRANT'S BEDROOM. TERRA-COTTA WOOD FRAMES AND IVORY MATS HELP UNIFY THE PRINTS, WHICH VARY IN SIZE.

KELLY USED COLOR COPIES OF A WORLD ATLAS TO DECOUPAGE THE FRONTS OF THE DRESSER DRAWERS, THEN PAINTED THE DRESSER DEEP GOLD.

Team effort

Designer Jenny Kennett understands that a sport is often more than a hobby for kids. A team activity like ice hockey may define the ebb and flow of a household's everyday life. Rather than let all that energy remain outside the home, Kennett wanted to capture the sport's excitement in an inviting living space. "When a child is involved in hockey, it involves the entire family," explains Kennett. "That's how this design came to be."

Two towering bunk beds establish a dormitory-style sense of communal space for four. The double-decker sleeping arrangement clears floor space while maintaining a designated personal area for each occupant. "Because we were dealing with such a big space and 10-foot ceilings, the twin bunk beds made a lot of sense," Kennett notes. "We wanted to give the impression that no family would be too big for this room."

A capacity for handling kids doesn't detract from the

TWO WHITE BUNK BEDS PROVIDE STATELY ELEGANCE IN A ROOM DEDICATED TO YOUTH AND SPORTS.

HOCKEY STICKS SERVE AS PLAYFUL DECORATIONS. A SOFT CHAIR AND RICHLY STAINED SET OF DRAWERS SET A MORE REFINED MOOD.

room's style. The beds' furniturelike details contribute to a sophisticated sensibility, as does an elegant dresser and grown-up armchair. The furniture's stained wicker balances a classic tone with a casual texture. Anticipating the energy—and school gear—of a roomful of hockey players, the desktop workspaces discourage excessive clutter. Intended to make tidiness simple and efficient, the beds' coverlets are made to slip easily into the bunks' side rails.

Amid all of this stylish function, the decor establishes a vibrant and playful sense of youth. A cartoon-inspired mural occupies an entire wall. Lighthearted and joyful, the painting provides levity without diminishing the room's subdued mood. "We specifically wanted the cartoon effect, not the colors, to set the tone and make it playful," Kennett says.

The hockey theme appears in unexpected places, seamlessly integrating the sports theme. For instance, the desk chairs feature combination hockey-stick and -puck backrests, and the embroidered pillows showcase hockey-theme slogans and images. Above the set of drawers, hockey sticks provide a sculptural wall hanging, while another stick serves as a curtain rod. The window's valance hangs from a broad, looping white rope, reminiscent of sturdy skate laces.

For Kennett, the clever fusion of classic style and boisterous youth is a natural part of putting together a creative and sensible space. "We wanted to see how far we could take the theme," she says. "And besides, why buy drapery rods when you can use hockey sticks?"

EMBROIDERED PILLOWS BUILD THE ROOM'S THEME WITHOUT DISRUPTING THE SUBDUED ATMOSPHERE.

A HOCKEY STICK IS THE NATURAL CHOICE FOR A CURTAIN ROD IN THIS SPORTS-THEME ROOM.

Classic Ride

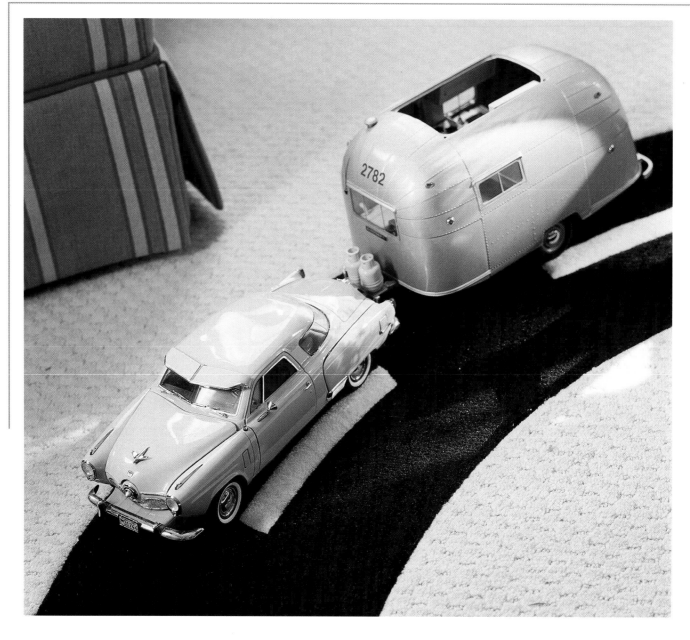

INTERIOR DESIGNER MELANIE MILLNER FOUND THIS VINTAGE CAR-AND-CAMPER PAIR ON EBAY.

SWINGING ARM LAMPS AND WALL-MOUNTED SHELVES PERFORM THE BEDSIDE FUNCTIONS NIGHT TABLES NORMALLY WOULD.

Little boys come home from the factory with all engines revving, so a bedroom inspired by vintage cars is the perfect place to garage their dreams of the open road. A duvet cover sprinkled with classic cars and trucks sparked interior designer Melanie Millner's interest in the theme. Her knowledge of her own young sons drove it home in this designer showhouse bedroom.

"I know how little boys think and play," Millner says. "I custom-made the highway rug because boys need a place to drive their cars other than the walls and furniture."

Before rolling in the vehicle accessories, Millner wanted to lay a sturdy groundwork. Neutral walls and floor covering highlight strong accent colors. "Black adds a sophisticated

Highway-inspired rug
Swinging bedside lamps
Road signs as wall art

Children can map their transcontinental journey on the bathroom's toile wallpaper.

Car-shape door pulls, hubcaps, and kid-size suitcases enhance the bathroom's journeying theme.

Vintage road signs and toys that coordinate with the room's color scheme add up to a classic look.

look, while red accents give the room some punch," she says. "When you combine strong colors like red, blue, and black with classic tailored lines, you create a good foundation that parents can adapt as the child grows."

In addition to classic colors, traditional furnishings such as simple bunk beds, a child-size club chair, side tables, and tailored window treatments give the room a grown-up air. In place of traditional art, Millner drove away with road signs from antiques stores and ordered rims and hubcaps from a vintage wheel supplier to adorn the walls. Old toys complete the setting.

"Children love the basic old toys," Millner says. "They will gravitate toward something old because it's interesting and different." Large and small cars and trucks and a miniature gas pump enhance the room's decor and encourage play.

The adjoining red-and-white bathroom is a notch above most pit stops. Toile wallpaper featuring U.S. maps serves as a backdrop for the smart white trim and cabinetry. Red ticking covers the window seat and Roman shades, and shiny hubcaps reflect the giddy faces of children eager to chart their next great adventure.

The Fun Factor

It's unusual for a small child to inspire a whole-house color scheme—but then again, Lucy Keim is no ordinary girl. When Beth Keim and her husband, Keith, adopted Lucy from China, they could see that her exuberant spunk deserved an equally spirited bedroom. "Since infancy, Lucy's had this fantastic, wide-open personality," says Beth, an interior designer. "Kids deserve a room that reflects their personality. Lucy picked the hot pink. She loves hot pink. In fact, Lucy is hot pink—it's bold and stands out, just like her!"

So it was that Lucy's room came to include pink fabrics, a pink dresser, and pink accents. Beth began, however, with inspiration drawn from a geometric-pattern rug. "That rug dictated everything," Beth says. "When I design a room, I like to start with one major item, like a rug or fabric, and

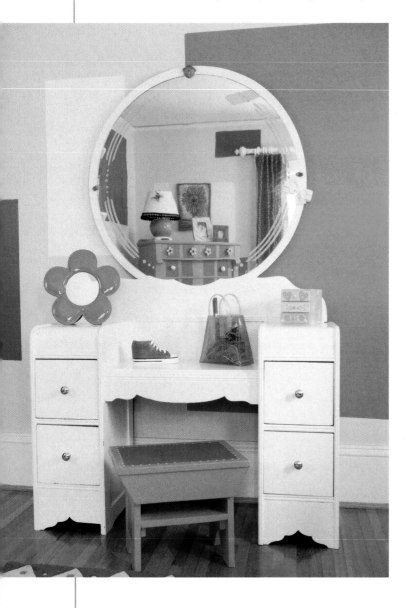

work my way around it. In Lucy's room I wanted the major punches to be on the floor and walls, and I wanted to keep the furniture simple."

Instead of choosing a small childlike pattern—which may have overwhelmed the large space—Beth painted sizeable squares and rectangles randomly on the walls. "When you tell someone you're painting big squares all over the walls, you can tell they're thinking, 'Oh, no!'" Beth says. "People are scared half to death by that kind of art. But when it works with everything else in the room, it's not so scary."

The geometric wall pattern pumps up the fun factor and will adapt as Lucy—and her collections and pictures—grows. "If you keep pattern to a minimum, or use it on a large scale like in Lucy's room, the walls won't fight with all of their personal things later," Beth says.

To balance and brighten the room, Beth painted most of the furniture glossy white—making it pop from the walls. The dresser, however, models a two-tone pink stripe treatment. It's just one of many furniture rescues that Beth incorporated into the room. Another is the thronelike bed. Each piece has the same design "feel" but brings its own character and uniqueness. "It feels great to resurrect a thrift-shop find that has great lines but is just a mess," Beth says.

For the boldly painted dresser, Beth substituted large white balls and yellow daisies for plain glass knobs. "I like to mix up knobs," Beth says. "For example, if you put daisy knobs on the entire dresser, it would detract from the fact they're daisies. If you use just a few across the top drawer, they stand out."

A few kid-friendly touches—including mom-and-daughter chairs for bedtime stories, shelves for doll display, and a closet transformed into a pint-size dressing room—inject a youthful liveliness.

Lucy's arrival transformed the Keims' lives—and she worked her magic on the family's home too. Beth and Keith switched out their sedate blues and browns for daring reds, oranges, and yellows after her arrival. It's a fun, kid-centered home for Lucy and little sister, Kate. "We knew her room needed a bold, bright palette to match her nature," Beth says.

BETH KEIM PAINTED A VINTAGE DRESSING TABLE WHITE. ALL OF THE ROOMS' ACCENTS INCORPORATE LUCY'S FAVORITE COLOR—HOT PINK.

BETH LOVES THE LINES IN THIS THRONELIKE BED. GREEN ACCENT PILLOWS COMPLEMENT THE BRIGHT-HUED BEDDING.

A CREAMY BASE BACKS UP THE LARGE WHITE, RED, AND ORANGE RECTANGLES AND SQUARES BETH PAINTED TO TIE THE WALLS TO THE ROOM'S PINK COLOR SCHEME. MATCHING CHAIRS IN DIFFERENT SIZES ACCOMMODATE PARENT-CHILD READING TIME.

LUCY KEIM READS FROM A FAVORITE TITLE ON HER BED. THE ROOM'S BRIGHT WHITE FURNITURE POPS AGAINST THE DEEP ACCENT COLORS.

Favorite books find a home in a four-tier rack. Beth custom-painted the kitchen set to match the color scheme.

Clever use of space made possible this dressing room closet, complete with storage space for favorite animals and books.

The suspended tea party ceiling is an upside-down version straight out of Wonderland. It comes complete with flowers, silverware, and take-out boxes. China pieces came from sets Beth collected over the years.

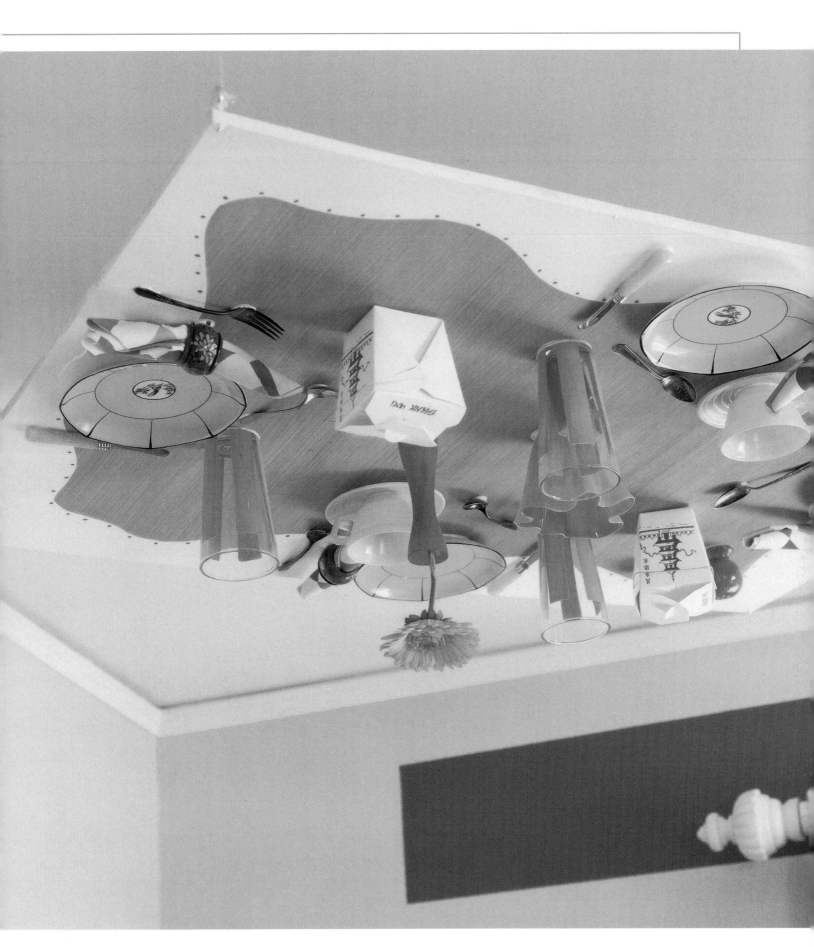

SHABBY-CHIC RETREAT

Stylish casual is the rule in Eliza Rosenberg's relaxing bedroom. Creamy yellow and warm white create a backdrop for bunches of cheery painted cherries. Cherries also appear on teacups stacked on two shelves and a diminutive, fabric-covered footstool. A fan of unmatched room design, Eliza's mother, Cathy, opted to fill the room with a mix of complementary pieces. A buttery yellow chest of drawers sits under the large window. Its white accents mesh with the room's many pieces of white painted furniture. Crystal knobs—some of them vintage, some new—help unify the look. Two nightstands flank the bed, but they aren't a matched set. Cathy chose pieces similar in size and shape for a shabby-chic, pulled-together look.

Over the years, Cathy and Eliza painstakingly selected vintage handkerchiefs to use as decoration for a personalized bedcover. Cathy then used a tight-stitch on her sewing machine to attach the squares to the bed quilt.

Each of the multilayer window treatments follows the room's cottage look. New pink and white-stripe ticking was used for the side panels. Curtains from Eliza's nursery provided the fabric for the top-layer valances, and rows of pom-pom fringe complete the treatments. On all the windows, Cathy elected to hang treatments inside the casings to allow the impressive molding to stand out. Even above the bed, a double-fringed valance flounces above framed quilt pieces to extend the window-rich feeling of the room.

THE FABRIC WINDOW TREATMENTS, DETAILED WITH A ROW OF POM-POM FRINGE, ARE HUNG INSIDE THE WINDOW CASING SO AS NOT TO DETRACT FROM THE WIDE MOLDINGS.

A PICKET FENCE BED TOPPED WITH A VINTAGE-STYLE QUILT CONTRIBUTES TO THE ROOM'S SUNNY APPEAL.

A DOUBLE-FRINGED VALANCE LIKE THOSE ON THE WINDOWS HANGS ABOVE THE BED. MISMATCHED LAMPS, PAINTED BEDSIDE TABLES, AND A CHANDELIER LEND FURTHER VINTAGE ELEMENTS.

CAR KID'S PARADISE

Six-year-old Tyler Lesch has a passion for cars. "It's a boy thing," says his mother Brenda. In fact, Tyler even points out the make and model of cars he sees on the road. His mother bought him an auto-theme bedspread, but he begged for more. So she decided to accelerate the car quotient.

Brenda used deep gray chalkboard paint over a backdrop of blue to create an elaborate road system that travels the room—complete with yellow divider lines. The main road circles at chair-rail height with vertical side roads evenly spaced throughout.

A black-and-white checkerboard pattern resembling a race flag speeds the theme along a primary-color scheme. The pattern covers the chair cushions, desk and dresser drawers, and mirror frame. Brenda made simple window shades from checked fabric lined with black. Red ribbon ties add a dash of color.

To complete the unified look, Brenda painted a thrift store desk and a new, unfinished dresser in primary colors. Start your engines!

THE WINDOW TREATMENTS ARE REMINISCENT OF CAR RACING'S CHECKERED FLAG.

A PAINTED SWITCHPLATE SHOWCASES THE COLOR SCHEME FOUND THROUGHOUT THE ROOM.

CHARMING, CAR-RELATED ITEMS SUCH AS A PARKING METER PIGGY BANK, TRAFFIC LIGHT, AND ROAD SIGNS ROUND OUT THE AUTO THEME.

Storybook Sweet

Far from Paris and a house covered in vines, a little girl's room pays tribute to the storybook character *Madeline*.

When it came time for 5-year-old Emma Sidman to make way for a baby sister and move into a grown-up room, her favorite storybook came off the pages and into reality.

Emma and her mom, Lauren Sidman, share a love for Ludwig Bemelman's story about an adventurous and endearing young girl living in Paris and saw the new room as the perfect opportunity to showcase their admiration.

Lauren enlisted interior designer Gretchen Edwards to lead the transformation. Edwards was not familiar with *Madeline*, but after reading the story, she immediately became inspired. "The very first page about the house with the vines made it roll," she says.

She began with that house, using it to make wooden window cornices, and continued with chairs and a child-size table decorated with the words from the opening passage of the book.

THE CUSTOM-MADE LAVENDER AND GREEN BEDDING WITH WHITE PIPING REPRESENTS THE ROOM'S COLOR SCHEME. PATTERNED THROW PILLOWS AND A BLACK-AND-WHITE CHECK HEADBOARD KEEP IT INTERESTING.

DESIGNER GRETCHEN EDWARDS BOUGHT THE TABLE AND CHAIRS AT A LOCAL RETAIL STORE AND PAINTED THEM WITH COLOR-COORDINATED VINES, GRAPES, AND CHECKS. FABRIC SLIPCOVERS SOFTEN TWO OF THE CHAIRS.

Edwards painted the opening passage from the book around the border of the tabletop.

Five-year-old Emma enjoys a relaxing cup of tea in her room.

The room exudes simple sophistication reminiscent of the French storybook setting. A model of the Eiffel Tower, a simple white lamp with a shade of white roses, and a flea market-find oil painting allude to fresh flower markets and France. The elegant tea setting allows Emma and her guests to enjoy classy French-style afternoons of talk and treats.

The curvy headboard, with fabric pinafore cover, adds a touch of pattern, movement, and French style, while *Madeline* dolls represent the captivating spirit of the character and her story.

Edwards used Emma's favorite color, purple, for the foundation of the room's color scheme. A soft, calming shade of lavender brightens the walls and most of the bed. "There are some scary purples out there," Edwards says. "This lighter tone is more sophisticated and easier on the eyes."

Solid greens balance the purple hues, while black-and-white check fabric on the headboard adds a subtle accent. Two of the chairs wear green slipcovers made from the same fabric as the bedding, a softening touch. The other chairs are handpainted wood.

"The room came together better than I could have imagined," Lauren says. Both Emma and Lauren love the end result, filled with the atmosphere and images of their favorite story. "I'm proud of how it turned out," Lauren says. "Even down to the accessories, it works."

Emma treasures her charming new room and the story that inspired it, and is sharing them both by reading *Madeline* to her little sister, Olivia.

THE WHITE DESK FEATURES A SMALL COLLECTION OF LIMOGES BOXES AND A CLASSIC WHITE LAMP. AN OTHERWISE PLAIN WHITE MIRROR IS LACED WITH A LAVENDER RIBBON. MADELINE HERSELF HAS A GOOD VIEW OF THE ROOM, PERCHED AS SHE IS ON THE DESK TOP.

THE WOODEN WINDOW CORNICES ARE A NOD TO THE OPENING PASSAGE OF THE BOOK, WHICH DESCRIBES AN OLD HOUSE IN PARIS COVERED WITH VINES. SHEER BLACK-AND-WHITE CHECK FABRIC PANELS ALLOW SOFT LIGHT TO SHINE THROUGH.

Traditional and Timeless

An elegant escape for a little lady, this spacious bedroom provides a private place for homework, entertaining, and daydreaming. The goal, says interior designer Tish Key, was to fill the space with "the beautiful things that will fill [the occupant's] life in years to come."

Great light and classic architectural details combine with a traditional approach and a soft pastel palette. The result is timeless and sophisticated. The focal point is a handpainted Italian bed topped with a canopy of cream-and-yellow check fabric that gathers in the center to form a rosette. The same classic checked silk makes a frilly vanity skirt, two stuffed chairs, and the floor-length drapery panels. Key decorated the bed with shams adorned with the child's embroidered initial and two hand-embroidered bolsters that emulate the headboard's graceful floral painting. A soft moss-color check pattern covers the ottoman at the foot of the bed. Windowpane-plaid carpet in sea-mist green ties the color scheme together.

Elegant details include an iron-and-crystal chandelier, a black marble and white wood fireplace, and an antique mirror with gilded ornamentation.

BUILT-IN BOOKCASES FLANKING THE WINDOWS PROVIDE AMPLE STORAGE FOR BOOKS, PHOTOS, AND STORAGE BINS. THE TUFTED LOVE SEAT NESTLED IN THE WINDOW IS COVERED IN A LUSCIOUS BUTTER-YELLOW LINEN VELVET.

SOFT COLORS AND CHECKED FABRICS UNIFY THIS SOPHISTICATED SPACE FOR A TIMELESS APPEAL.

Handpainted Italian bed topped with silk canopy

Checked patterns used throughout

Elegant details including a chandelier and fireplace

CRAFT TIME

In this fanciful room, a little creativity goes a long way. Rather than using an outside designer, this family applied their own ideas and talents, making the room a grand project in which parents and daughter served as designers and artists. Capitalizing on the child's vivid imagination and a bit of crafty parental insight, this space blooms into an exuberant garden full of youthful joy.

Exhibiting the vigor of a creative youngster, the color palette explodes with vibrant, intense colors. Bright pink, sunny orange, and pastel green establish an energetic mood and build the room's garden theme. Handpainted flowers rise up the walls, sporting brilliant orange petals and pink polka dots. A simple giant flower growth chart dominates one wall, its blossom center framing a photo of the room's inhabitant. Even the window shade displays a painted scene of flowers on a green background.

Clever details contribute unexpected amenities and help

A PAINTED MIRROR SPOTLIGHTS THE STAR OF THE SHOW.

AN ABUNDANCE OF FLOWERS AND COLORS FILLS THIS FANCIFUL GARDEN-INSPIRED BEDROOM.

MAGNETIC WALL PAINT
CHILD'S ORIGINAL DRAWINGS ON BEDDING
WINDOW SHADE AS UNEXPECTED CANVAS

Believe
in Magic

build a creative atmosphere in this crafty space. Personal drawings affixed with iron-on transfers grace the bedcover in a quiltlike design. Small pockets sewn on pillows welcome favorite dolls and mementos, while a parade of clothespin fairies dances along the edge of a lampshade. An interactive feature that keeps it forever fresh and new: Magnetic paint ensures the walls readily welcome art, notes, photographs, or simply the quaint ladybug magnets that appear to crawl around the room.

The design includes plenty of frills and ruffles to nurture a young girl's sense of glamour. Encased by glittering pink fabric, a small table serves as an irresistible vanity. Beveled glass on the tabletop protects a changing array of favorite photos and paper keepsakes. Thanks to the wall's magnetic paint, green picture frames welcome a rotation of hand-made artwork supported by magnet clips.

With stars that grace the curtain rods and giant blades of grass in place of wainscoting, this bedroom design inspires imagination. Each exuberant detail possesses personal meaning and represents a family project. Overflowing with color and individual touches, a little creative effort truly gives this girl a one-of-a-kind room that is entirely her own.

STARS, FLOWERS, AND RIBBON ADORN THIS PLAYFUL WINDOW TREATMENT, WHICH INCLUDES SHEER FABRIC CURTAINS AND A HAND-PAINTED SHADE.

A FEATHER BOA-FRAMED MIRROR HANGS ABOVE THE PINK VANITY TABLE. STACKING BOXES STASH EVERYTHING NECESSARY FOR PLAYING DRESS UP.

A FLOWER PAINTED ON THE WALL ILLUSTRATES MARISSA'S GROWTH. MAGNETIC PAINT HOLDS A FRAMED PICTURE AT THE FLOWER'S CENTER.

3 TEEN RETREATS

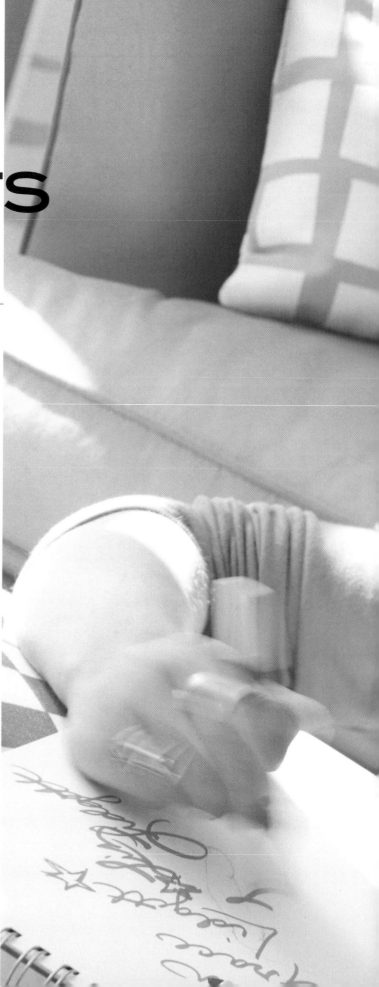

Any teenager say the perfect bedroom is one that's private—no parents or younger siblings allowed. Storage for books, memorabilia, CDs, and, of course, clothing is vital to any teen room. Space for hanging out with friends or doing homework is a big issue, but as important are the aesthetics of the space. To create the ultimate escape, allow your teen to infuse his or her room with personal style. That might involve bold colors, animal prints, butterflies, sports memorabilia, or guitars. A successful venue will draw your daughter's friends for slumber parties and gabfests or your son's buddies for hanging out and talking shop. Even better, it will keep your teen happy until he or she leaves the nest.

FUNKY FINISH

Packing big-time style into a small space is easy when bold colors and groovy graphics are used as a starting point. Just ask interior designers Amy Weinstein and Jeffrey King, who took the color cues for this showhouse bedroom from the punchy palette of a poster that hangs on the wall.

Wide horizontal stripes in varying colors and sizes ring the walls of the 10×9-foot room. The stripes add color and depth without overwhelming the small space. "Paint is extremely important because it's a small room," Weinstein says. "It was fun to play with that sort of color combination, to bring it out in all the different sizes and widths of stripes. It gives the room some pizzazz."

A challenging layout, including a full wall of glass doors, didn't stop the designers from pairing key bedroom elements with funky finishing touches. A large bed would have dominated the space, so Weinstein pushed a twin against the wall lengthwise and placed a king-size headboard behind it. The low bed and headboard combine to create a sitting and sleeping area that exudes modern simplicity.

Near the bed, a full-size table with chairs hosts card games, homework, or friends. "I think it's human nature to gather around a table," Weinstein says. "A round table 'floats' in the room; you can move around it. It allows for more flexibility than a desk pushed against the wall."

A multipurpose study corner stores books, a laptop, and other daily necessities on shelves off the floor. A sleek CD rack travels up one wall, fulfilling a storage need in a fun, yet practical way. "In a small room, you need to use your vertical surfaces as much as possible and get things off the floor," Weinstein says.

The designers succeeded in creating a laid-back contemporary space that suits a growing boy or a college student. "Kids want a place of their own that's both a personal escape and a place to be with friends," Weinstein says. "As a designer and parent, I want the room to look good and function well. This room does both."

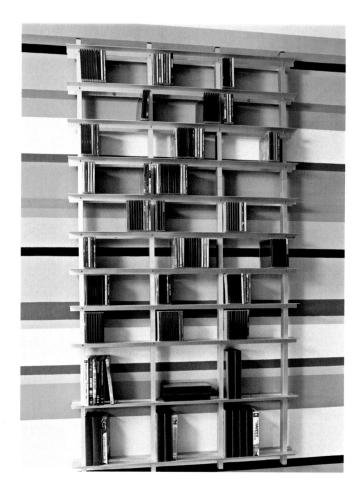

A WALL-HUNG CD RACK PROVIDES PLENTY OF
STORAGE SPACE FOR MUSIC AND MOVIES AND ADDS A
SCULPTURAL TOUCH TO ONE OF THE ROOM'S WALLS.

A LARGE BED WOULD HAVE DOMINATED THIS TINY
ROOM, SO DESIGNER AMY WEINSTEIN OPTED FOR A
TWIN BED TURNED LENGTHWISE WITH A KING-SIZE
HEADBOARD BEHIND IT FOR DAYBED-LIKE SITTING.

Next to the bed, a wicker ottoman and low, sturdy shelf provide a space for working on a laptop. The shelf doubles as a bedside table and, along with the rest of the shelves, fits with the room's clean, contemporary design.

With little room for a full-size desk, the table offers plenty of room to study and doubles as a space to hang with friends. A hip white fixture overhead reinforces the contemporary atmosphere.

TEEN DREAM

When teenage girlfriends come to call, they require plenty of space for sprawling out. In Anna Grace Barry's bedroom, two twin beds, a window seat, a cushy chair, and a built-in desk provide ample room for teen talkathons and slumber parties. Classic decorating decisions mean the room will retain its style throughout Anna Grace's teenage years.

A monochromatic color combination of cream, white, and peachy pink sets the sophisticated tone. Multiple patterns embellish everything from wallpaper to carpet, lending a whimsicality and sense of fun. Both Anna Grace and her mother, Amy, selected colors and patterns. "I wanted something that was young but also sophisticated because kids grow up so quickly and their tastes change so much," Amy says.

They went with built-in storage and seating without sacrificing floor space. Separated by an antique nightstand, twin beds with cream-color metal frames rest side by side on one wall. A petite upholstered chair accompanies the window seat.

The window treatments garner lots of attention. Anna Grace wanted to ensure her room was dark for sleeping, so designer Linda Knight Carr created layered, feminine curtains topped with elaborate valances. Four curtain panels lined with black fabric can be drawn over the large windows to shut out light. Above, the decorative valances include a layer of ruffles that echoes the plaid pattern found on the window seat and a top layer made from the fabric used on the nearby settee.

The mix of colors and patterns is soothing and mature, yet decidedly girlish as well. "Her room has a real peacefulness. The colors are very calming," Amy says. "It's a great place to retreat from the world at the end of a busy school day."

CUSTOM-MADE CURTAINS AND VALANCES FRAME THE LARGE WINDOWS. THE BUILT-IN WINDOW SEAT AND AN UPHOLSTERED CHAIR ARE PERFECT SEATING FOR ANNA GRACE AND HER FRIENDS.

LAYERED DECORATIVE VALANCES
BUILT-IN WINDOW SEAT WITH STORAGE
SOPHISTICATED AND SIMPLE COLOR SCHEME

TWIN BEDS SIT SIDE BY SIDE IN ANNA GRACE'S BEDROOM. THE SIMPLE COLOR SCHEME RECEIVES A BOOST FROM FEMININE DETAILS INCLUDING PLAID BED SKIRTS AND GOLD-FRAMED PAINTINGS SUSPENDED ON SILK RIBBONS.

THE BEDS AND THE BUILT-IN DESK ARE PAINTED THE SAME CREAM COLOR AS THE ROOM'S TRIM. SHELVES, DRAWERS, AND CUPBOARDS PROVIDE PLENTY OF STORAGE. A LENGTHY BULLETIN BOARD ACCOMMODATES PHOTOS AND MEMENTOS OF TEEN LIFE.

Contemporary Cool

In a sleek home, a typical little boy's room just won't cut it. So when Christy and Todd McCain set out to decorate the bedroom their sons share, they bypassed cars, trains, and superheroes in favor of functionality and fun.

"We wanted the room to last for several years," Christy says. "The boys were small when we decorated it, so we wanted to do a room that would take them through middle school—something that was masculine-looking but cool."

The inspiration for the room's color scheme came from the polka-dot fabric that covers large headboard pillows

FUN AND WORK COME TOGETHER ON THIS WALL, WHERE THE KIDS CAN SHOOT HOOPS OR DO HOMEWORK. THE DESK FEATURES METAL FILING CABINETS AND A PAINTED DOOR.

THE MCCAIN BOYS' ROOM IS BOTH SOPHISTICATED AND PLAYFUL. PILLOW "BALLS" BRING IN A ROUND ELEMENT AND ENCOURAGE A CASUAL ATMOSPHERE.

on each bed. The palette introduces touches of red, which are present throughout the house. Black, blue, and silver round out a harmonious neutral combination.

Black headboards allude to the rest of the home's clean-lined design and include niches the boys can accessorize with different items, depending on what they're into at the time. The beds themselves sit low to the ground, in part so the McCain's then-young sons wouldn't hurt themselves if they tumbled off while playing. Black canvas fabric attached to inexpensive blue comforters enhances both size and style.

With such simple bedding, it's no trouble for the boys to make their own beds, plus cleaning requires only a washing machine.

Interior designer Beverly Baribault wanted the kids to be able to swing from the curtains—literally. The black canvas window treatments hang from heavy-duty grommets on a galvanized fence post.

"I think the best thing about that room is it really is functional for kids yet sophisticated enough for the adults—a lot of kids will have a room that's functional but the parents

Designer Beverly Baribault made sure the curtain rods would hold up should the young McCain boys swing on them. The rod is made of galvanized fence post, and heavy-duty grommets hold the panels in place.

The storage drawers between the beds are actually metal filing cabinets. The beds sit low to the ground, a feature which promotes bed-making and ensures neither brother will be hurt when they play around.

can't stand to go in there," Baribault says. "Even the parents enjoy this room."

In fact, Mom contributed her own personalized touches to the space, sewing tasteful monograms into the boys' pillows and creating the artistic compositions above the nightstand.

Some of the most inexpensive elements are also the most remarkable. Low metal filing cabinets that previously inhabited Todd's office now serve as a bedside table. Additional filing cabinets make up the base for the desk, the top of which is constructed from a hollow residential door painted red. On the wall above the desk, extra large clips purchased at an office supply store display the boys' latest artwork.

A surprise decoration hangs near the desk—a full-size basketball hoop and backboard. Baribault decided to incorporate the hoop after envisioning pillow "balls" as a way to bring a soft, round element to the room. Now the boys can challenge one another to a pickup game in their own bedroom or just sit in bed and shoot hoops.

PILLOW "BALLS," AS WELL AS SMALL RUBBER BALLS, ARE CORRALLED IN A WASTEBASKET NEXT TO THE DESK FOR IMPROMPTU PICKUP GAMES.

CHRISTY MCCAIN IS A FAN OF TASTEFUL MONOGRAMS. SHE DESIGNED THE ELEGANT COMBINATION THAT PERSONALIZES HER BOYS' SHEETS.

HEAVY-DUTY CLIPS FROM AN OFFICE SUPPLY STORE CREATE EASY-TO-CHANGE DISPLAY SPACE ABOVE THE DESK.

STORAGE WITH STYLE

Barbara Mullane's son, John, spent more than a decade in a cramped room devoid of personality, before it became clear that a little boy's nursery wouldn't work for her growing son. Enter designer Susan Andrews, who came with plans for a bold room loaded with colorful details fit for a teen and chock-full of storage elements any mother would love.

The palette is a far cry from the primary combos that typically color boys' rooms. Marine blue and tangerine orange form a punchy color combination that doesn't overpower when paired with subdued khaki.

Barbara and John agree the bed is the highlight of the space. "We love the bed with the giant pullout drawers underneath. It's probably one of my favorite things," Barbara says. "And John really uses the drawers—they're filled."

The pullout drawers are actually three wooden boxes mounted on utility casters so they roll under the bed for easy accessibility. Decorated with bright blue paint, khaki radiator inserts, and large handles, the storage receptacles stow everything from games and toys to clothing and bedding.

Another easy option, ready-made cubes are stacked together and affixed to casters to serve as a movable unit. Some of the resulting cubbies are left open, while others have blue-painted doors with galvanized metal inserts that hide belongings from view.

The same blue-and-metal combination that graces the storage elements is found in the window treatments. Because John's room is located on the home's second story, where total privacy is not an issue, Andrews chose to create playful blue shutters that cover only the lower half of the windows. The radiator metal inserts block views while allowing some light to filter through.

"I wanted to give the room a bit of an industrial edge by using the metal on the storage cupboards and shutters and the casters on the drawers," Andrews says. Along these lines, a sheet metal insert backs the closet door, serving

STORAGE BOXES WITH UTILITY CASTERS AND METAL HANDLES FIT UNDER THE BED, TUCKING JOHN'S BELONGINGS OUT OF SIGHT.

THE SHUTTERS' METAL RADIATOR INSERTS WERE CHOSEN FOR THE STAR PATTERN'S MASCULINE, SLIGHTLY RETRO LOOK. BECAUSE THE BEDROOM IS ON THE SECOND FLOOR, THERE'S NO NEED TO COMPLETELY COVER THE WINDOWS.

ORANGE TWILL VALANCES WITH INDUSTRIAL ZIPPERS MATCH THE ORANGE TWILL STRIPES AND PILLOWS ON THE BED. A GAP BETWEEN THE CURTAINS AND SHUTTERS ALLOWS PLENTY OF LIGHT.

An industrial-style lamp is positioned to shine light on a blue chair in the new reading corner.

Designer Susan Andrews removed the mirror on the back of the closet door to make room for a sheet metal bulletin board.

as a message center that displays invitations, awards, and reminders.

Above the shutters, orange twill valances with rugged zippers up the middle are attached with metal hooks and grommets, furthering the industrial scheme. Andrews used the same orange twill to decorate the duvet and three large pillow shams. Blue letters on the pillows spell out John's initials. "John loves to stack his big pillows up and lay in bed reading," Barbara says. "It's kind of like his own sanctuary now. Every kid needs a private, personal space, and that's what this has become."

The collegiate theme took shape as Andrews designed the space and is most evident in the dresser. Decorative painter Tina Blanck covered most of an unfinished dresser with a warm stain, then painted an imprecise plaid pattern on the front of the drawers, picking up the plaid that borders the

pillows on the bed. University pendants painted over the plaid complement the collegiate-style tone-on-tone letters on the walls.

With its bold colors, innovative storage options, and university-inspired theme, John's room is sure to suit him through high school. In fact, Andrews says John might even consider taking some of the elements from the room with him to college. "Now he has a much more grown-up look that he can definitely grow with for a long time," she says.

Big, Bold, and Beautiful

A bold personality deserves a bold room. Designing with a teenage girl in mind, Atlanta interior designer Kay Douglass decided against girly-girl walls and furniture, and opted for something more flexible. Her goal was to take this girl from her teenage years into adulthood.

Douglass painted the walls with large wraparound stripes in two saturated shades of orange. The stripes underscore the room's size and set a vibrant, warm, and energetic tone. "I went with saturated colors," Douglass says. "Pastels would have been too wimpy."

And she didn't stop there. Hot pink enlivens the bed linens, adorns the chairs' upholstery, and accents the striped window drapes and rug textiles.

To complement the burst of pinks and oranges, Douglass opted for oversize bright-white furnishings and trim. "Against the color, the white shapes pop right out and get noticed," she says.

But color isn't the only standout here: The canopy-shaped wrought-iron bedframe and the oversize floor lamps warrant attention too. And an elegant sitting area sports an unusual roller skate table lamp. Although most of the room is quite grown-up, an antique rocking horse adds a fun touch, reminiscent of a time not long gone.

THE STRIKING BED, FURNISHINGS, AND OVERSIZE GRAPHIC FLOOR LAMPS STAND OUT AGAINST THE BOLD ORANGE-STRIPED BACKDROP.

ABSTRACT PAINTINGS AND TWO ORANGE CHAIRS DEFINE A SMALL SITTING AREA NEAR THE BED. THE LAMP IS MADE FROM ANTIQUE ROLLER SKATES.

STRONG, SATURATED COLOR CHOICES
BOLD-SHAPED OVERSIZE FLOOR LAMPS
FLEXIBLE DESIGN FOR CHANGING TASTES

Thoughtful details can take a room halfway around the world. Evoking the atmosphere of distant exotic lands, this small bedroom transforms a teen's love of adventure and animals into an imaginative refuge. "When she was 10, I asked Alexandria what she'd like in her bedroom, and she said, 'jungle,'" recalls Tina Barclay, Alexandria's mother and the room's designer.

Tina set her sights on a room in which a hint of British Colonial style establishes an exotic sensibility along with an element of elegant timelessness. The wallcovering establishes a cozy hut feel and makes a striking, multidimensional presentation. Rugged blinds repeat the bamboo look on the windows, while lush tassels dangle from pointed curtain rods.

Reminiscent of a protective canopy, sheets of linen descend from a tin crown high on the wall and sweep over a classic sleigh bed. "I don't like to do theme rooms because they don't stand the test of time," Tina says. "But we talked about it and came up with the idea of a tree house above the jungle floor. I used more formal fabrics for a British Colonial look that she wouldn't tire of."

Lush fabric and classic details initiate an enduring style, but the design maintains a playful disposition as well. Animal print pillows, curtains, chairs, and duvet spark the imagination and render the space visually intriguing. A bright ceiling mural features tropical leaves and a mischievous lemur who peeks through a bamboo opening.

Even with the safari theme, this space offers flexibility for the inevitable changes in taste. The ceiling mural exudes youthful charm but is easy to paint over as interests mature. Earth tones of gold and sage green transition easily into adult years. The tropical combination creates an attractive, comfortable balance that blends time-tested style and colorful vision. "Alexandria's 12 now," Tina says, "and she still loves it. She feels like she's in her own little tree house up in the sky."

A CANOPY-LIKE LINEN AND CLASSIC SLEIGH BED LEND ELEGANCE AND MATURITY TO A YOUTHFUL JUNGLE-THEME SPACE.

THICK TASSELS HANG FROM THE DRAPERIES, AN EXOTIC YET SUBDUED DETAIL.

Bamboo blinds and animal-print draperies contribute to the room's theme while offering an earthy, mature color palette.

A ceiling mural imbues the space with playful color, softening the room's more classic features.

The window sheds light on a mix of subdued green tones and animal prints, establishing a tropical atmosphere.

Sharing a bedroom is never easy. But when the roommates are two teenage girls and the space is small, things can get downright ugly. Clever storage and a dose of upbeat, fun-loving color ensures peace and harmony.

The modest budget for this bedroom redo dictated that big-ticket items—including traditional poster beds and contemporary dressers—be reused. The beds run parallel to each other, and the dressers pull double duty as storage units and benches at the foot of the beds. The beds' comforters with lots of color and pattern help pull together the furniture pieces' mismatched styles.

The comforter also pointed to the choice in wall color—a fresh green—which sets a playful tone. Red and blue work as accents, as do the yellow and orange accessories.

The furniture arrangement divides the room into two separate areas, ensuring each sister has her own space to lounge. A bold striped runner divides a blue area rug, further defining the space, while a painted metal cabinet between the two beds is wide enough to share as a nightstand. The girls agreed to sacrifice one of two closets to gain a study space, which easily converts back to a closet, should the need arise.

The sisters learned how to extend the life of a budget by using bargain fabrics, an assemble-yourself desk, and a re-upholstered armchair. Fabric motifs inspired the painted tree that "shades" the armchair as well as whimsical elements such as the tulip art and the metal bird finial on a metal bucket-turned-lampshade. It all adds up to quirky style and a happy coexistence for two teen sisters.

Inexpensive letters spell out the room's unique arrangement and function.

A striped runner defines the middle ground between two sisters' beds. The nightstand's shiny yellow finish is courtesy of an auto-body shop.

A TREE WENDS ITS WAY UP THE WALL, ITS BOUGHS
FRAMING THE TOP OF A NEWLY UPHOLSTERED
ARMCHAIR.

A DRILLED HOLE IN THE BOTTOM OF A METAL BUCKET
TURNS AN ORDINARY HARDWARE STORE FIND INTO A
FUN LAMP.

The girls' study tucks behind doors lined in blue linen. A pair of inexpensive cabinets provides each girl with space to call her own.

Magnets secure photographs, cards, and mementos to metal trays that attach to the wall with mounting strips.

Road Culture

Designer Jenny Kennett had a particular kind of teenage girl in mind when she envisioned this hip bedroom. "She's comfortable in her jeans; she's a little funky; she's athletic; she likes her music," muses Kennett. "She's comfortable with her femininity, but everything around her doesn't have to be feminine."

In tune with this groovy girl's personality, a dramatic evocation of mid-20th-century Americana transforms an ordinary bedroom into a trendy retreat. Using the classic Airstream trailer as inspiration, Kennett's nostalgic design fuses the energy of rock 'n' roll with the liberating romance of the open road. "Today everything retro is so in and cool," Kennett says.

In order to evoke a vintage trailer appearance, the bedroom's previously unremarkable walls now boast a metallic silver paint and thin strips of riveted molding. A distinctive luggage rack stretches the length of the ceiling and provides the extra storage an active teen needs. Setting a hip retro mood, a corner banquette partners with a steel diner-style table that inspires conversation. The rounded ceiling mimics the Airstream's famous curved form and completes the room's homage to an American road classic.

The caravan style is heavy in metallic tones, so Kennett chose vibrant shades of green, suggesting both youthful energy and vintage style. Green carpet coordinates with the bedding's citrus forms and tree patterns that cover pillows and curtains. Decorative details such as glass bottle vases, beaded fringe, music memorabilia, and a color-coordinated lava lamp build this room's groovy nostalgic mood. The funky color fusion continues into an adjacent bathroom where lime-green glass tile establishes a glowing atmosphere.

The tone may be funky, but the design is intended to be flexible. Richly toned brown furniture grounds the youthful decor in a foundation of maturity. Generous cushions take the place of a headboard. The bed turned sideways against the wall creates the inviting impression of a couch. A corner desk organizes favorite magazines, personal mementos, important books, and the inevitable homework.

Visually intriguing and structurally innovative, this room's vibrant character suits the confident and creative teen. Like the era it evokes and the trailer it emulates, it's infused with the spirit of adventure. The design invites the occupant on a remarkable journey of self-discovery; a long, strange, and ultimately wonderful trip.

LIME GREEN AND DEEP BROWN ARE THE RETRO COLORS OF CHOICE. SOME OF THE PILLOWS ON THE BED ARE COVERED IN THE SAME GREEN-TREE FABRIC AS THE WINDOW TREATMENTS.

A BED TURNED SIDEWAYS AGAINST THE WALL GIVES THE IMPRESSION OF A SOFA. A LUGGAGE RACK ALONG THE CEILING MAKES GOOD USE OF UNEXPECTED STORAGE SPACE.

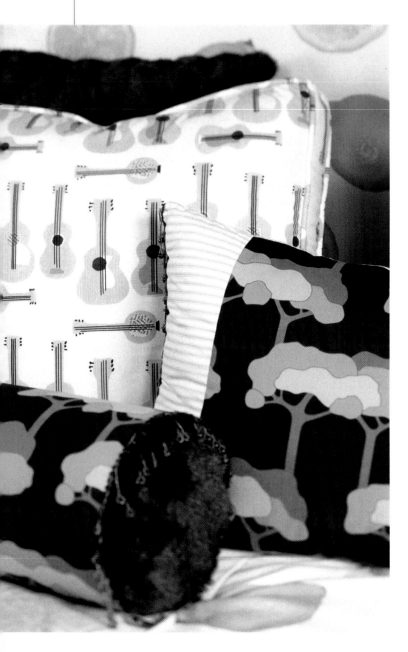

Decor mimicking classic Airstream trailers

Corner banquette as hip seating area

Trailer-style luggage rack

A CORNER DESK OFFERS PLENTY OF STORAGE
AND DISPLAY SPACE FOR A TEENAGER'S FAVORITE
POSSESSIONS.

A ROUNDED CEILING AND DINER-STYLE BANQUETTE
ESTABLISH A RETRO CHIC AMBIENCE.

SHINY METAL FURNISHINGS, INCLUDING THE RETRO
DINETTE TABLE AND PANTRY SHELVES, ARE A NATURAL
FIT IN THIS ROOM.

ECHOING THE BEDROOM'S COLOR PALETTE, THE
ADJACENT BATHROOM'S FLOORING AND WALLS BOAST
LIME-HUED GLASS TILE.

THE SHOWER CURTAIN POCKETS MAKE A DESIGN OF
REFLECTIVE CDs.

Curtain Cool

Simple solutions often lead to the most sophisticated results. Designer Megan Jowdy's goal was to fashion a changeable design that was out of the ordinary without being flashy. "I wanted this room to be soft and feminine," she says, "but I didn't want it to be a typical girl's pink room."

An unhindered swathe of drapery ensures the room's uncommon beauty. With curtain rod supports every six feet along the ceiling, sheer organdy panels soften the room in a flowing, diaphanous elegance. Covering the windows as well as the walls, the white panels feature a design of delicate pale blue flowers that seem to sway in the breeze. The cloth may hang over doorways and windows, encouraging an enclosed intimate ambience, or it may be tied back with thick, tasseled cords. "It's both a wall treatment and a drapery," Jowdy says.

White furniture and crisp white cotton bedding enhance the room's dreamy mood. Mismatched furnishings include modern lamps and a traditional armoire, both decked out in bright white as a means to create a unified, timeless appearance. Inexpensive slipcovers give second life to the beds' original headboards and further the room's theme. The result is a clean, undisturbed harmony. "It makes everything cohesive," Jowdy says.

Touches of blue, drawn from the drapery's pale blossoms, offer a soothing counterbalance to the expanse of white. The indigo blankets provide a cool natural tone that grounds the space without disturbing its airy ambience. An inviting powder blue chair ties the combination together in a subtle pattern. The connected bath's brilliant azure wallpaper sets a serene tone that connects the two spaces with a common color theme.

Just as the panels and furniture are deceptively simple, Jowdy's choices of wall decor present a pleasing minimalism. An impressive six-foot-tall mirror leans against the wall, at once offering a space-enhancing element and a

BLUE AND WHITE DRAPERIES GO BEYOND THE USUAL BORDERS TO PROVIDE THE BASIS FOR A SIMPLE RETREAT.

DRAPERIES COVERING ALL OF THE WALLS

SIMPLE BLUE AND WHITE COLOR PALETTE

TALL, ELEGANT MIRROR

COVERING DOORWAYS AND WINDOWS, THE BEDROOM'S
CURTAIN WALLCOVERINGS PROVIDE AN INTIMATE
TRANSITION TO AN ADJACENT BATHROOM.

OFFERING A REFLECTIVE CONTRAST TO THE FABRIC
DRAPES, AN ELEGANT SIX-FOOT MIRROR TAKES THE
PLACE OF ARTWORK ALONG ONE OF THE WALLS.

way to break up the dominant expanse of curtains. "It takes the place of artwork," explains Jowdy. The understated theme continues with portraits of flowers mounted directly through the drapery onto the walls.

The serene elegance of basic colors and simple decor delivers an attractive level of flexibility. The inhabitants may remove the curtains as tastes evolve and partner the predominantly white color scheme with new colors. The pictures of flowers are actually painted photocopies, a simple, inexpensive, and easily replaced element. "In two years, if the girl is tired of flowers, she can make copies of buildings in New York," the designer says.

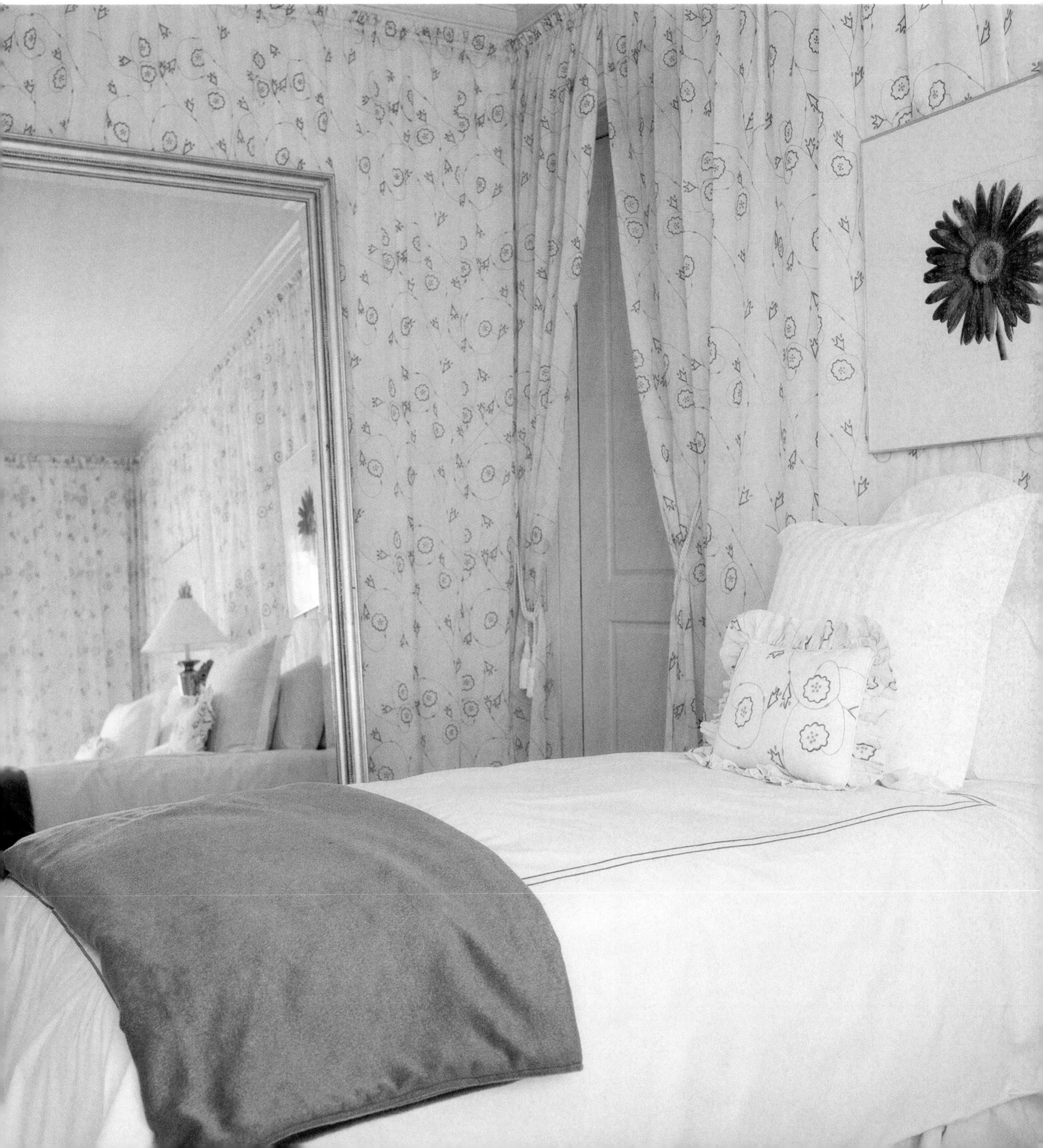

THE PILLOW SHAMS BRING THE DRAPERY DESIGN TO THE BEDS. THE MOSTLY WHITE COLOR SCHEME RESULTS IN A UNIFIED SPACE.

A SOFT BLUE CHAIR AND WHITE ARMOIRE LEND
SOPHISTICATION WITHOUT DETRACTING FROM THE
LIGHT-AS-AIR PRESENTATION.

SIMPLE PORTRAITS OF FLOWERS EASILY TRADE OUT
FOR SOMETHING ELSE WHEN THE ROOM NEEDS TO
BE REFRESHED.

Black Is Back

An open mobile shelving unit stands coolly against a wall or may be moved to center stage as a room divider.

A horizontal black and white Beatles poster repeats the shape of the headboard and sings a hip retro tune.

For a mother who loves white walls, a teen's request for black sounds like a design death sentence. But incorporating black into a bedroom color scheme isn't as hard as it seems, according to designer Jodi Mensing. In fact, done right, black earns major design points from parents as well as teens.

"Kids are looking for things that make them feel special," Mensing says. "They want a room that doesn't look like all of their friends' rooms."

The key to pulling off a black room is balancing its potency with three things: bright white, super-charged colors, and a bit of metal for shine. Mensing split the walls in two by screwing a metal chair rail into them. Brilliant sky blue lightens the ceiling and the walls below the chair rail. Up top, black chalkboard paint covers three walls and vibrant green livens the other. Mensing calls this green contrasting wall "a power wall," and says it's a respite from the black expanses.

Funky patterned fabrics and accessories also jazz up dark spaces. The metal bed wears a zigzag-textured green bedspread and a puffy blue comforter. Patterned pillows incorporate the black, white, green, and blue palette. A white modular shelving unit and a silver entertainment center add brightness. Both are on wheels, so they're easy to move to different parts of the room if desired.

At floor level, a squishy green beanbag chair and graphic pillow make a convenient place to sprawl with a book or talk on the phone with a friend. For more formal seating, a structured armchair sits next to a rug beside the video game center.

Clean-lined black, white, glass, and chrome accessories keep the look cool. A multifaceted star pendent lamp shines above the bed, while a black and silver lamp on the tri-level bedstand encourages late-night reading.

Black doesn't have to be dark or boring—mixed with the right colors and elements, it's a stylish element in a teen's modern retreat.

THANKS TO THE USE OF BLACK CHALKBOARD PAINT, THE UPPER HALF OF THREE WALLS SERVES AS MESSAGE CENTERS. THE METAL CHAIR RAILS ARE MAGNETIC SO THEY'RE NATURAL PICTURE-HANGERS.

A STUFFED BEANBAG CHAIR IS THE PERFECT SPOT FOR PLAYING THE GUITAR OR RELAXING WITH A BOOK. THE WHITE CUBBY-STYLE SHELVES STORE RECORDS, BOOKS, AND MEMENTOS.

Versatile black bins slide into the modular shelving, keeping clutter contained.

Cotton Roman shades have a modern feel and an interesting texture.

Inexpensive metal strips screwed into the wall form a magnetic chair rail great for posting pictures or notes.

His Favorite Things

Teenager Brandon James's room is a direct reflection of his style and interests. Favorite color? Blue. Passion? Music. Frequent Saturday-morning pastime? Accompanying his mom to flea markets and yard sales, which helped Brandon develop a love for the look of the early 1970s. "The inspiration for my bedroom was the music I was listening to at the time and the fact that blue was, and is, my favorite color," Brandon says.

Big stretches of blue paint, bedding, and carpet embolden the space. Two broad stripes follow the perimeter of the room and serve as a backdrop for the color scheme. A large blue rug softens the dark hardwood floor. Vintage '70s-era pieces collected on Saturday morning jaunts with Mom to yard sales and flea markets furnish the room: a credenza-turned-dresser, an armchair, a bench covered in a funky multicolor pattern, and a globe. Two midcentury Eames chairs (also popular in the '70s) flank the fireplace. Music-theme prints, matte-chrome beds, white miniblinds, and other period-appropriate accessories represent Brandon through and through.

BLUE AND WHITE STRIPES DOMINATE THE ADJOINING
BATH AND COORDINATE IT WITH THE BEDROOM.

FLUFFY FAUX-FUR PILLOWS FROM A LOCAL HOME
CENTER SOFTEN THE ROOM'S RETRO STYLE.

BRANDON'S PERSONALITY SHINES THROUGH HIS
MADE-TO-SUIT BLUE-HUED BEDROOM.

SEPARATE STYLES

A big rectangular bedroom became a teen dream suite thanks to a handy partition made of inexpensive home center materials. "Privacy is a big issue for teenagers," says Melissa Kleve, a University of Nebraska-Lincoln student who designed the room with classmates for the Omaha Symphony Showhouse. "None of us liked it when our parents walked into our rooms. The partition creates a sitting area near the door, and a sleeping area behind it." Light flows through the partition, which features smooth sheet metal and plastic panels over a 2×4 frame on one side, and corrugated metal and plastic panels on the other.

The students heated the room's industrial look with color, drenching three walls with midnight blue and the other in deep orange. On the floor, hard-wearing cream-color Berber carpet texturizes and lightens, while an inexpensive square of black automobile carpet deepens the scheme. A galvanized metal channel mounted on the wall becomes a continuous display shelf, running the length of the room and linking both sides of the suite.

PLASTIC PANELS ALLOW LIGHT TO FLOW THROUGH THE PARTITION, WHILE METAL PANELS MAKE AN ATTRACTIVE BACKGROUND FOR MAGNETIC WORDS.

BOLD COLORS TURN UP THE SUITE'S VISUAL HEAT. CUSHY CHENILLE SPREADS AND ANTIQUE IRON BED FRAMES PROVIDE TEXTURAL CONTRAST TO THE PARTITION'S STEEL AND PLASTIC.

Sheet metal-covered coffee table

Metals and plastic on a divider wall

Separate sleeping and lounging areas

Hot Hues

Traditional elements become modern when they fill a bedroom for a funky young woman. "I wanted this teenager to have both current things and also a connection to the past," says designer Christina Dutton.

Barely-there pink walls accessorized with white trim produce a soft blush that makes the furnishings pop. A circa-1915 brass bed with a new gleaming brushed nickel finish renders charm without looking too cute. The tailored hot pink bedcover decorated with a floral flush taken from the retro fabric on a nearby chair contrasts beautifully with a midnight black bedskirt. Pink sheers running on ceiling tracks act as a modern-day take on a dreamy bed canopy.

The 1950s armchair has a pink, yellow, and black covering that inspired the kicky color scheme. A yellow and pink checked rag rug softens a dark wood floor. A sun-kissed adjacent bathroom runs with the happy hue, thanks to a yellow and white stripe vinyl floor, buttery yellow walls, and lemony curtains.

A STYLIZED FLORAL DESIGN IN MONOCHROMATIC YELLOW DECORATES THE VANITY SURFACE.

SHINY PATENT LEATHER AND PINK-PIPED UPHOLSTERY TRIM GLAMORIZE AN ART DECO DESK CHAIR.

A CONSOLE TABLE-TURNED-VANITY SHOWS A LITTLE LEG WITH A SKIRT HUNG INSIDE THE TABLE'S EDGE.

THREE-DIMENSIONAL STARS FILL THE HEARTH OF THE BEDROOM'S FIREPLACE. TWO LARGE WINDOWS FLANK THE MANTEL, ALLOWING NATURAL LIGHT TO DRIFT THROUGH THE SHEER PINK CURTAINS AROUND THE BED.

Suite Sixteen

The key to 16-year-old Christina Dorobek's sophisticated bedroom is grown-up glamour. Thanks to the help of interior designer Catherine Bailly Dunne, the fun, fresh two-room suite is "definitely my dream room," Christina raves.

Color ties the bedroom, sitting, and work spaces together. Easy, breezy hues with Swedish country flair—including light green, lavender, and sea blue—are youthful yet not childish. A four-poster bed frame draped with sheer fabric strikes an elegant but easygoing tone.

"Keeping the colors youthful while using more mature furniture helps this room work well for the long haul," Dunne says. "Christina won't tire of it and neither will her mom, who can use it for a guest room when Christina's away at college."

The queen-size bed features custom-made, color-coordinated linens. "The fabric is serene and simple, more elegant than childish," Dunne says. "It had the right sophisticated air without being too trendy or cute."

Christina's involvement in the planning resulted in sweet dreams for both teen and parents. Mom and daughter selected everything for the room together. "Letting her choose her own fabrics and furniture meant that it was really her room," Christina's mother, Julie, says.

CUSTOM-MADE LINENS AND ACCENT PILLOWS COMPLEMENT SHEER LAVENDER WINDOW AND CANOPY PANELS.

THE VANITY IS A MISMATCHED ELEMENT THAT FITS WELL DUE TO A COMMON AURA OF ELEGANCE.

IN A NOD TO THE TYPICAL TEEN ROOM, THE BACK OF CHRISTINA'S DOOR IS COVERED IN STICKERS SHE HAS COLLECTED.

Bali Beautiful

A celebrity's four-poster Bali-inspired bed prompted teenager Catherine Barton to turn her little-girl space into a hip teen retreat bursting with vibrant color. Her parents, Kim and Lee, enlisted interior designer Stephen Pararo to help re-create the space.

Pararo draped Catherine's antique four-poster bed with wisps of bright tie-dyed sheers in a modern blaze of fuchsia, orange, and red. Together the old and new elements capture this in-between stage of her life. "I think it gives it a blend of young and old that's perfect for a teenager," Pararo says.

Other pieces bolster this cool young adult look. The dark Jacobean dresser features a carved S-scroll design that appeals to Catherine's modern sensibility, while a rustic log chair upholstered in funky patchwork fabric represents her folksy side. A bead-edged table skirt with energetic splashes and drizzles of paint shows off her artistic influence. Even the paisley pattern on the draperies and dust ruffle is hip. "This is a very modern, updated, artistic rendition of a very traditional idea," Pararo says of the pink, purple, and gold fabric. "It gives the room a light and whimsical feel."

One big plus: Catherine can reuse some of the more traditional furniture, including the bed and dresser, when her style matures.

A TABLE ACCENTED WITH A BEAD-EDGED SKIRT AND SPLASHES OF COLORFUL PAINT ACCOMMODATES AN EQUALLY FUNKY CHAIR.

COLORFUL SILK PILLOWS FEATURE DIVERSE TEXTURES AND DESIGNS.

VIBRANT TIE-DYED SHEERS MODERNIZE THE TRADITIONAL FOUR-POSTER BED.

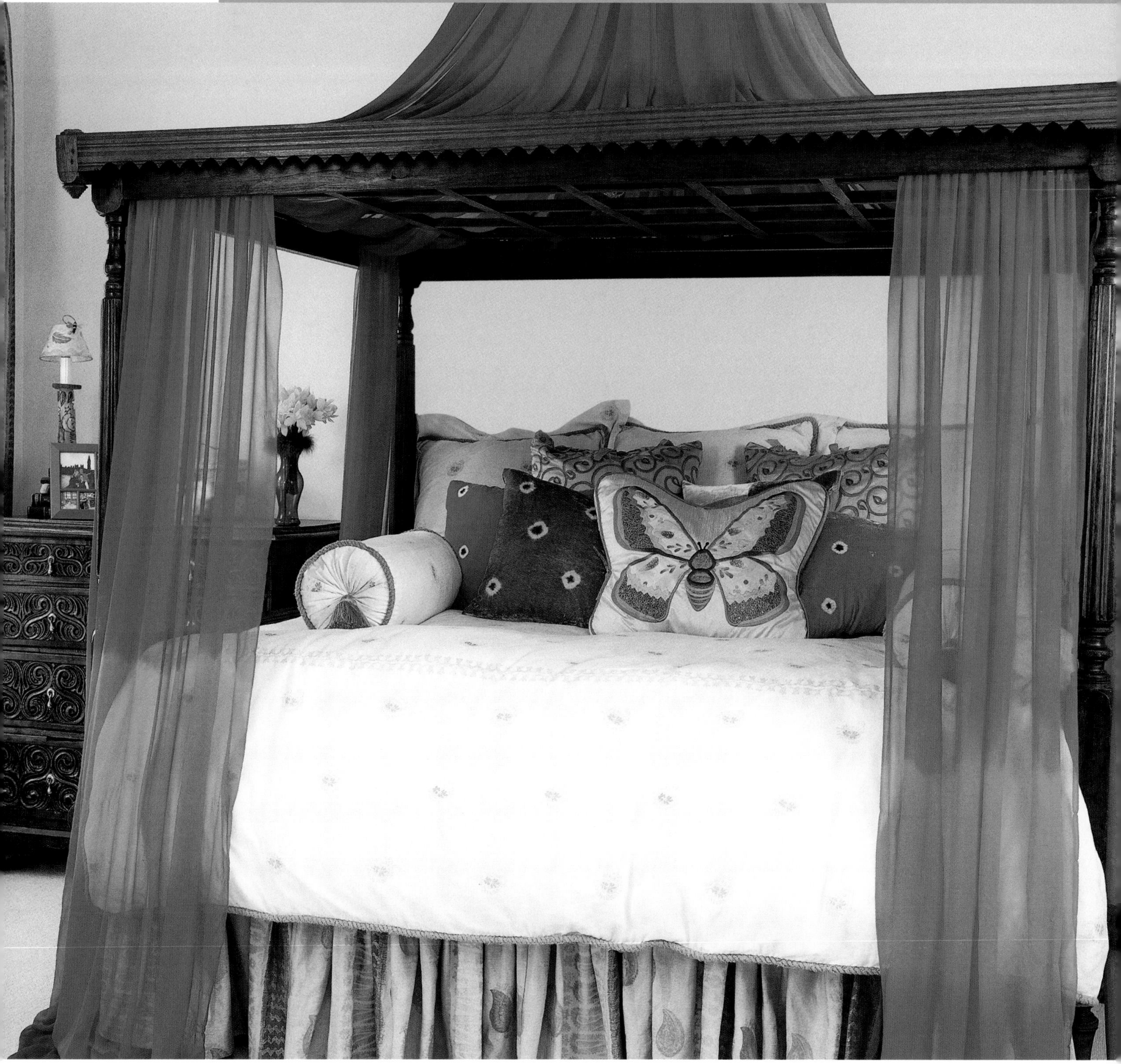

4 BATH-TIME FUN

In children's soapy, sudsy bathtime worlds, the only necessary ingredients are bubbles and laughter. Beyond these requirements, the bathrooms in this chapter illustrate the many faces of kid-friendly design. In your child's bath consider the practicalities first. Is it worth it to install shorter sinks children can reach and lower shower fixtures that cater to youngsters? Or will a well-placed stool and an adjustable showerhead do the trick? As with any space tailor-made for kids, remember to make it fun. Paint is the easiest and most affordable way to customize a bath to your child's tastes. Whether you're going for bold color or fanciful details, you can work wonders with vibrant towels, inspired toothbrush holders, and a child's original wall art—elements that are easy to switch out as tastes change.

Playful Patterns

Banish a boring bathroom by mixing patterns, colors, and textures. This girl's bath, awash with yellows and pinks, playfully combines dozens of checks and dots, assorted stripes and squiggles, a miniature mural, and a few bouquets of flowers. Paint leaves its mark on every square inch—even the sink, freestanding re-enameled tub, and radiator are canvases for multicolor designs, a mural, and polka dots.

Decorative painters brushed, rolled, and daubed on the merriment, creating a dreamy world well suited to young imaginations. Gold bath fixtures, a chandelier, and other accessories garner a rich look, while yellow, pink, and white glazes transform existing wall tiles into a cheerful checkerboard. Squiggles and squares unify the pattern-rich theme. Should a new child move in, a slight tweak in the palette—think blues, greens, and reds—is all that's needed to make the space more masculine.

Even the baseboards, window frames, and door jambs became artist's canvas in this bath.

A floral fabric replaces traditional under-the-sink cabinets and ties together the pink and yellow palette.

194

A PLETHORA OF PATTERNS
MINIATURE MURAL ON THE TUB
CLASSIC GOLD BATH FIXTURES

Pampered in Pink

Sure, a pristine white and chrome bathroom may seem chicly spalike to your average adult, but most kids would prefer a powder room with more punch. This once all-white bathroom comes alive with hot pink walls and do-it-yourself cottage details in shades of pink, pool blue, and grass green—custom-made to pamper the preteen girl who primps here.

The shower curtain—actually a striped bedsheet topped with a coordinating floral valance that's edged in piping and a narrow ruffle—supplies texture and movement. Buttonholes sewn through the layers provide openings for rings accented with bejeweled refrigerator magnets.

For a matching effect, the curtain and valance fabrics are used as a patchwork border on the custom bath rug made from two bath towels with batting in between. The same fabrics also serve as decorative patches for the room's towels.

Floral refrigerator magnets accent metal shower curtain rings.

This hot pink bathroom with bright cottage accents is sure to please any little princess. The comfy bath mat with a patchwork edge was made from two towels.

BATH IN BLOOM

There's never a groggy morning in this South Carolina bath. Filled with fun and frivolity, the design energizes thanks to sunny color, celebratory flowers, and snappy accents.

"I love the cheerful look of the bathroom," says homeowner Laurie Thornhill. To decorate the basic white space, friend and decorative painter Gray Mixson covered the walls with pale yellow paint, which causes the white fixtures to visually pop.

She then painted on '70s-style flowers and insects for a lighthearted feel. To create the freehand images, Mixson first painted the basic forms using latex paint, then added colorful details to distinguish ladybugs and dragonflies.

The cheerful daisy pattern is repeated throughout the bathroom on hand towels, bath mats, and drawer pulls. A yellow and white checkered valance, finished with a sizable blue tassel, dresses the window in a way that allows sunlight to stream through.

THE BLUE DAISY BATH MAT INSPIRED THE ROOM'S SCHEME. THE MOTIF BLOOMS ON THE WALLS, HAND TOWELS, AND EVEN THE DRAWER PULLS.

HANDPAINTED FLOWERS AND DRAGONFLIES FURTHER THE LIGHT, CHEERFUL MOOD.

THE VALANCE, A YELLOW AND WHITE CHECK TRIANGLE, PLAYS UP THE BATH'S SUNNY STYLE AND MAKES A POINT WITH A PLUMP TASSEL.

SIMPLE DAISIES PAINTED ON WALLS

YELLOW GINGHAM WINDOW TREATMENT

GLASS-TOPPED SHOWER TO WELCOME IN LIGHT

ALL-AMERICAN BATH

In Zach Murtaugh's bed and bath suite, rustic furniture and accessories rule the roost. When they decorated their son's new room, Melinda and Mark Murtaugh focused on his love of camping, fishing, and sports. They knew they couldn't go wrong with a red, white, and blue color scheme. "He's just an all-American boy," Melinda says.

But the Murtaughs also wanted to make sure the room could age with Zach, then six years old. "I wanted to establish a basic style that could be changed little by little as [Zach and his sister, McKay,] get older," Melinda says.

To ease the boy's transition to preteen and beyond, the Murtaughs kept the American theme simple. In the bathroom, Melinda used blue to unite the space with the adjoining bedroom. Blue and white striped wallpaper is subtle and boyish. The custom vanity features wood countertops and an antiquated blue finish. "All the beating up on it just adds character," Melinda says.

On the countertop, jars corral toothbrushes and cotton swabs. The model ship is a souvenir from a trip to Cape Cod. Mom and Dad joined forces to create the patriotic vanity mirror. Mark constructed the frame, and Melinda painted the stars and stripes.

The bathroom's rustic style spread to the bedroom in the form of a mix of handmade, flea market, and store-bought furniture. A Craftsman-style bed frame, mirror made from an old horse harness, and rustic ladder that serves as a place to hang extra blankets during sleepovers individualize the space. Zach even had a say in the palette—it was his idea to paint the bedroom ceiling blue with yellow stars.

Regardless of Zach's age, his bedroom and bathroom will remain all-American cool.

ZACH'S RED, WHITE, AND BLUE BATHROOM FEATURES A FLAG-TASTIC MIRROR THAT HIS PARENTS BUILT AND PAINTED THEMSELVES.

THE BATH'S PATRIOTIC THEME SPREAD TO THE BEDROOM, WHERE RUSTIC FURNITURE PAIRS WITH STARS AND STRIPES.

COORDINATED BEDROOM AND BATH THEME

HANDPAINTED FLAG MIRROR ABOVE THE SINK

CUSTOM VANITY WITH ANTIQUATED FINISH

JUST DUCKY

The yellow rubber ducky has been a fixture of many childhood bath times, and this brilliant water closet pays homage to the timeless toy. The amusing waterfowl found nesting throughout the room simultaneously delivers storybook charm and comic relief.

Towels, toys, and slippers feature the familiar orange-billed character. A handpainted step stool, sunshine mirror, and white wicker storage baskets display a classic nursery school sensibility. Ducky drawer pulls and a pedestal sink establish a comforting, nostalgic aura.

Coordinating with the classic toy's appearance, radiant shades of yellow produce a sunny ambience. Golden

A HOODED DUCK TOWEL AND A PILLOW SIGN REFLECT THIS BATH'S YOUTHFUL NATURE.

GLOWING GOLDEN TONES EMBODY THIS SUNNY BATHROOM'S HOMAGE TO THE CLASSIC RUBBER DUCK TOY.

wainscoting and lemon-tone walls illuminate the bath while mellow white borders provide crisp definition. The pedestal sink and linen shelf soften bold colors with a clean white presentation. A pleasing duck painting epitomizes this room's cheerful disposition and helps confirm that, as the song says, the rubber ducky does, indeed, make bathtime lots of fun.

Even the painted footstool has all its ducks in a row.

This child's play pail, a nostalgic element, introduces touches of red and blue that mellow the bold yellow tones.

Duck knobs adorn a drawer that stashes bathtime toys and towels.

POP ART PRIVY

Surprising accessories find a place in Catherine Barton's bathroom, which features a teenager-meets-traditional style. Designer Stephen Pararo helped the teen personalize her white-painted cabinets, brass fixtures, and triple-arched windows with bright colors and artisan accents. An apple green antique bench replaced an upholstered window seat, and funky handcrafted mirrors reflect Catherine's style. "We tried to accent with pieces that would be considered functional pop art," Pararo explains.

The bathtub curtains take a modern approach, hung from small medallion knobs rather than an ordinary rod. Jewelrylike curtain tiebacks made from glass beads and wire hold the fabric away from the tub. Hung high enough above the tub to avoid water damage (the shower is separate), a painting of a modern bed of tulips makes a cool statement in an unexpected place.

A POP ART PAINTING SUSPENDED ABOVE THE TUB STAYS DRY BECAUSE THE SHOWER IS IN A SEPARATE COMPARTMENT.

SMALL MEDALLION KNOBS REPLACE AN ORDINARY SHOWER CURTAIN ROD.

THE GREEN ANTIQUE BENCH MADE MORE COMFORTABLE WITH COLORFUL PILLOWS EXPRESSES CHARACTER AND OFFERS EXTRA SEATING.

Quack Factor

What's a mom to do when her child's bath has white flooring, white trim, a white sink, white accessories, and white walls? Brush it up with playful paint treatments that reflect the fun of splashing in the bathtub.

The casual stripes on the lower part of these walls came about thanks to a streaky application and intentionally imperfect edges. The technique lends the room a laid-back air and makes the treatment much more fun to do.

A yellow border stenciled with the beginning of a cherished nursery rhyme floats along at chair rail height. Color-washed blue upper walls become a pond for a line of adorable yellow duckies hatched with the help of a simple stencil.

A plain white sink and white storage elements pair with basic orange towels and a yellow bath mat, allowing the paint scheme to take center stage.

A FAVORITE BATHTIME RHYME ADDS A PERSONAL TOUCH TO BATHROOM DÉCOR.

CURLICUE FEATHERS AND TAILS INCREASE THE LITTLE BIRDS' ENDEARING QUALITY AS THEY SWIM ACROSS THE BLUE WALL.

YELLOW ACCESSORIES SUCH AS THE WINDOW SHADE, BATH MAT, AND HAND TOWELS TIE TOGETHER THE UPBEAT THEME.

NURSERY RHYME-STENCILED BORDER

IMPERFECTLY PAINTED VERTICAL STRIPES

BRIGHT YELLOW ACCENTS

rub a dub dub · rub a dub dub · rub a dub · rub

Attic Oasis

Teens love the modern look, and this bath proves that contemporary, clean lines can result in warm, comfortable styling. Awash in white, this attic bathroom gets a boost from cool art and colorful accessories. A freestanding tub and nearby vessel sink with a simple wooden base are simplistically modern. The white porcelain gleams when light streams through skylights cut in the ceiling.

A floral abstract hung low on the wall serves as the bath's focal point, lending an illusion of grandeur to the small space and inspiring an infusion of colors throughout. Accessories such as plush terry towels stored in a wall niche across from the tub, a soft blue bath mat, red and pink contemporary wastebaskets, and miniature bottles perched on the vanity mirror enliven as accents. The wood floor emits an allover inviting warmth.

SOAPS, BATH OILS, AND BOOKS WITHIN EASY REACH ENSURE A WEARY TEEN CAN UNWIND AFTER A LONG DAY AT SCHOOL.

PLUSH TERRY-CLOTH TOWELS IN SOFT COLORS DOUBLE AS ACCENTS.

POPS OF COLOR IN THE LARGE FLORAL PAINTING ON THE WALL AS WELL AS IN THE TOWELS STORED BY THE TUB INFUSE THE SIMPLE WHITE BATHROOM WITH PLENTY OF ENERGY.

VESSEL SINK WITH WALL-MOUNT FAUCET

FOCAL POINT PAINTING

TOWEL NICHE BUILT INTO THE WALL

Eye-Hopping Hues

Like a growing number of parents-to-be, Kate and Wayne Hood passed on the pastels and even sidestepped the primary colors, opting instead for a high-octane chartreuse hue to color their daughter's nursery. Pairing it with a soft pink hue in the adjoining bathroom makes a unique, utterly delightful color combination. "I wanted bright," Kate says. "I've read that bright colors are good for a baby."

Though interior designer Liz Williams went out on a limb with the eye-popping color, she played it safe with a baby-friendly motif: bunnies. A fanciful fabric dotted with pink, blue, and lavender bunnies used in the adjacent bedroom set the design in motion, inspiring the larger painted bunnies that hop along the nursery walls. A bunny welcomes all at child's-eye level, just outside the bathroom door.

The pink gingham walls, visible upon entering the nursery, entice curious visitors to peer inside. Details deepen the interest: Williams had the mirror frame painted with pink and green and found pink bunny knobs to round out the theme. A slim bookcase painted chartreuse matches the bedroom walls and maximizes storage space.

A LARGE PAINTED BUNNY ENTICES VISITORS TO ENTER THIS CHILD'S BATHROOM.

A SLIM BOOKCASE MAXIMIZES STORAGE SPACE AND ECHOES THE BEDROOM'S BRIGHT CHARTREUSE.

A PAINTED MIRROR FRAME, PINK BUNNY KNOBS, AND PINK GINGHAM WALLS PRODUCE AN EFFECT THAT'S SOFT AS SLIPPERS.

BOUNCING BUBBLES

Kids of all ages delight in boisterous bubbles. Dynamic blue-green walls set the stage for an exciting underwater adventure, where a bubbly random polka-dot pattern matches dotted shower tiles. The plaid floor tiles further the festive color scheme.

To prevent the room from becoming too busy, the trim, tiles, and shelving remain plain and white. Pristine white shutters control the generous window's infusion of light, offering the option of complete privacy. A glass shower enclosure upholds an open plan, making the room feel larger.

Accessories expand the color scheme. Yellow stars lend excitement to an ordinary step stool, stacks of towels in a built-in shelf make a pastel rainbow, and a potted plant boasts unexpected yellow and black stripes.

PAINTED SPOTS ON THE WALLS AND BATH TILES

PLAID FLOOR TILES

EASY-TO-REACH CUBBIES ABOVE TOILET

WHITE WOODEN TRIM AND WHITE BATHROOM
FIXTURES OFFSET BRIGHT MEDITERRANEAN BLUE
WALLS AND PATTERNED FLOOR TILES.

DUOTONE DOTS SEEM TO FLOAT ON THE WALLS,
ESTABLISHING A PLAYFUL AIR.

THE SHOWER'S BOUNCING BUBBLES INSPIRED THE
UNIQUE PAINT SCHEME.

215

HEAVENLY HERITAGE

Grand Victorian architecture may offer charm and elegance, but as Mike and Sumi Almquist discovered, it doesn't accommodate the needs of modern parenting. While restoring their 1893 home, the couple realized they needed to take the old structure and make it baby friendly. "It was inefficient, awkward, and full of unused space," recalls Sumi. Looking forward to the children in their future, the couple fashioned an entirely new bath that recognizes parental necessities without detracting from their home's heritage.

A 1930s-style tile provides the room's visual interest. A dappled white honeycomb design covers the floor, while a pale yellow tile with a trim of black forms the room's wainscoting. A buttery decorative trim frames a towering mirror and the counter's edge. White walls, cabinets, and a farm-style sink brighten the golden tone and establish an antique atmosphere.

Though the bath boasts vintage elegance, it still suits the life of a busy family. "We preserved as much of the original feel as we could while adding the modern conveniences they desired," says project manager John Lorange. An inspired half-wall barrier with curtains lets a shower become a visual attraction. Its capped divider matches the tile that tops the counter. A broad stand-alone sink addresses the needs of a new parent as it delivers a substantial fixture to the bathroom's appearance. Wide enough to comfortably fit an infant and fitted with an extendable kitchen-style faucet, the basin makes baby bath time safe, contained, and simple. "Moms love that sink," says Sumi.

The blend of modern and period style finds a pleasing balance in this new space. While an antique claw-foot tub provides nostalgic comfort, contemporary radiant heating warms the floor for small feet. As interior designer Steve Long notes, "The Almquists wanted the house to nod to the past but not be restricted by it."

COUNTERBALANCING THE ROOM'S VINTAGE AMBIENCE, THE BLOCKISH UNADORNED SINK PROVIDES A HINT OF MODERN STYLE BENEATH A TOWERING TILE-FRAMED MIRROR.

DEEP SINK BASIN WITH KITCHEN FAUCET

HALF-WALLS AROUND THE SHOWER ENCLOSURE

VINTAGE STYLING LIKE REST OF THE HOME

HALF-WALLS PROMOTE AN OPEN ATMOSPHERE. ELEGANT TILE EDGES TOP OFF THE SHOWER'S HALF-WALLS AND FRAME THE TILE SURROUNDS, BUILDING A SENSE OF UNITY.

AN ANTIQUE CLAW-FOOT TUB COMPLEMENTS THE HOME'S HISTORIC HERITAGE. THE HANDHELD FAUCET IS A CHILD-FRIENDLY OPTION.

Going In Circles

Any child will tell you: Drawing inside the lines is no fun. So when residential designer David Root found himself drawing the plans for a home on a circular lot, instead of playing the straight and narrow, he saw it as an opportunity to build a rounded home with a central turret. The gentle lines and sweeping curves affect everything, including the layout of a bathroom for the family's two young children. "The challenge was to fit a bath into the circular shape," says Root.

Two of the bath's walls curve. The inside wall arcs around the central tower. The parallel exterior wall follows the outside curve of the home. While doors and drawers are straight, the granite countertop curves along the vanity's

front and back edges, reinforcing the room's arc. The bath's granite deck also tapers gently inward from the exterior wall, though the bath itself is a standard shape. By eliminating a shower curtain, Root ensured that, until they are independent enough, kids can receive showering help from adults, while a long floor drain next to the tub catches any overflow from playtime splashes.

To lighten the lower-level room and provide a unifying element to vanity and tub spaces, Root installed five small square windows high on the exterior wall. A row of four windows floats above the two elliptical vanity sinks, while the other opens to the bath area, placed in a tiled enclosure behind a graceful arched opening. Root custom-built clear-finish maple cabinets in rounded shapes to fit along the curved wall and included a wardrobe-like storage unit for stowing towels, toys, and toiletries. "The cabinet boxes ended up being somewhat wedge-shape," Root says.

Wide maple moldings around windows and mirrors promote the Craftsman style found in the rest of the new home. Lighthearted kid accents include the sea creature tiles in subtle white relief and ocean-inspired drawer and door pulls in translucent colors. The room, like ocean waves, is always in motion with curves, and that inspires kids of all sizes.

STARFISH AND SEA HORSES TURN SIMPLE DRAWER AND DOOR PULLS INTO KID-FRIENDLY DECORATIVE ELEMENTS.

BOTH EXTERIOR AND INTERIOR WALLS CURVE. THE EDGES OF THE COUNTERTOPS, TUB DECK, AND BUILT-IN CABINETS FOLLOW SUIT.

Curved vanity to match curving room
Translucent colorful drawer pulls
Sea creature accent tiles

FIVE SMALL SQUARE WINDOWS PLACED UP HIGH FOR PRIVACY FOLLOW THE CURVE OF THE EXTERIOR WALL. THEIR MOLDINGS MIRROR CRAFTSMAN-STYLE DETAILS FOUND IN THE REST OF THE HOME.

BOLD MAPLE CABINETRY FOLLOWS THE GENTLE CURVE OF THE EXTERIOR WALL. THE TALL CABINET PROVIDES PLENTY OF KID-FRIENDLY STORAGE.

TIMELESS TILE

This bath, made to grow with a 4-year-old girl, features a classic checkerboard tile pattern that culminates in a geometric mural reminiscent of a wall-hung quilt. While the feminine yellow and pink reflect the child's current interests, the designer blended other warm colors to achieve quilt-like and timeless quality.

A sit-down vanity is a fun setting for a game of dress-up now and a serene place to apply makeup when she's older. A tile frame lends an arty edge to a standard mirror above the sink. Though the child uses only the tub to bathe now, the designer installed a showerhead for future use. A shower curtain or glass doors can come later.

To temper the colorful tile design, the bathroom fixtures, vanity, and wicker laundry basket are all white.

THE VANITY AREA BOASTS PLENTY OF DRAWER SPACE AND A TILE-FRAMED MIRROR.

A COMBINATION OF TILE TRIMS DRAWS ATTENTION TO THE WINDOW AND VANITY MIRROR. THE FLOOR, COUNTERTOP, AND WALL TILES OFFER COLORFUL DURABILITY.

LIKE A WALL-HUNG PATCHWORK QUILT, THE TILE MURAL CREATES AN AREA OF INTEREST ABOVE THE TUB.

Something Fishy

This bath embraces an imaginative underwater theme that invites children to take a journey beneath the waves. Playful schools of fish are irresistible to young snorkelers. One school swims at child's-eye level—on the lower half of the wall under a starfish border tile chair rail. Another floats underfoot. A brightly colored fish-shape net catches the eye and serves as a toy receptacle, making bath cleanup fun and easy.

The predominantly blue palette provides a rich, comforting ambience and builds the marine theme. Soft and warm to touch, a thick, indigo rug takes the wall's blue paint to a darker level. Translucent blue globes catch light by the window and suggest rising bubbles beneath the sea. A charming striped chair welcomes a small body. With underwater friends swimming all around, the combination of brilliant color and fanciful details makes this room a visually stimulating space for any undersea adventurer.

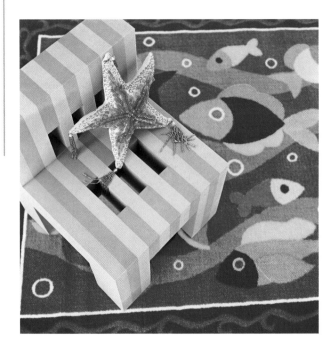

A water-resistant kid-size chair and thick absorbent rug make bathtime fun and comfortable.

Colorful fish images on the wainscoting tiles set the room's charming undersea theme.

Brilliant colors and fanciful fish images transform bathtime into an imaginative adventure.

When John Baldwin began renovating a bathroom for his son, Shawn, he wanted the room to be both welcoming and practical for the growing young man. "I wanted this to be a safe bath for Shawn and a fun place to be so he would want to wash up and brush his teeth," John says.

To accomplish that, designer Sally Dixon Martin chose fixtures that suit Shawn now and in the future. The double vanity set at mid-range height is sized to fit Shawn even as he grows. Easy-to-reach cubbies below the medicine cabinet allow for display of treasures, toys, and towels. The extra sink provides space for friends that spend the night—and a sturdy step stool ensures dad's help isn't required to reach towel bars.

Martin chose a tub that's convenient for both father and son: Its shorter sides make it a snap for Shawn to step into and out of and a comfortable height for John to assist when necessary. The tumbled marble floor mosaics reduce the danger of slipping and hide any dirt the youngster brings in. The adjustable-height handheld shower spray helps Shawn keep himself—and the tub—rinsed clean.

The shower is another place for Shawn to exercise his ever-increasing independence. A shower bench encourages Shawn to suds up feet, and niches in the walls allow him to easily reach soap and shampoo. A shower curtain is a safer enclosure than a glass door, and levers—in the tub, shower, and at the sink—are super simple for kid operation.

John enlisted Shawn's help in the decor, too: He chose the design and placement of the animal accent tiles that, along with the off-white tiles, replaced the original gloomy blue-gray terrazzo. After all the planning and work, John received the best compliment a parent could hope for. "[Shawn] loves it so much, and kids who come to play line up to use this bathroom too," he says.

The mid-range height vanity enables a growing boy to brush his teeth and wash up without dad's help.

Noah's ark and his animals brighten a variety of off-white tiles.

An adjustable shower spray encourages a growing boy to rinse the tub when he's done.

PINK PARTY

Evoking the age of bobby socks and poodle skirts, black, white, and shades of pink set the mood. Rich bubblegum tone wainscoting dominates the space, while painted bubble-like polka dots accentuate the white wall. Even the footstool, terry-cloth rug, and wastebasket are candy coated with incandescent shades that project energy and sweetness—perfect for any fashionable girl on the go.

Reinforcing the theme, wooden letters affixed with ribbon bows spell out the word "bubbles" along the wall. A white chest and black-and-white check tile floor provide cool counterpoints to the radiant ambience. The nostalgic color references to pink sweaters and saddle shoes broadcast a sugary homage to the sock hop and soda fountain, proving that pink poodles appeal to every generation.

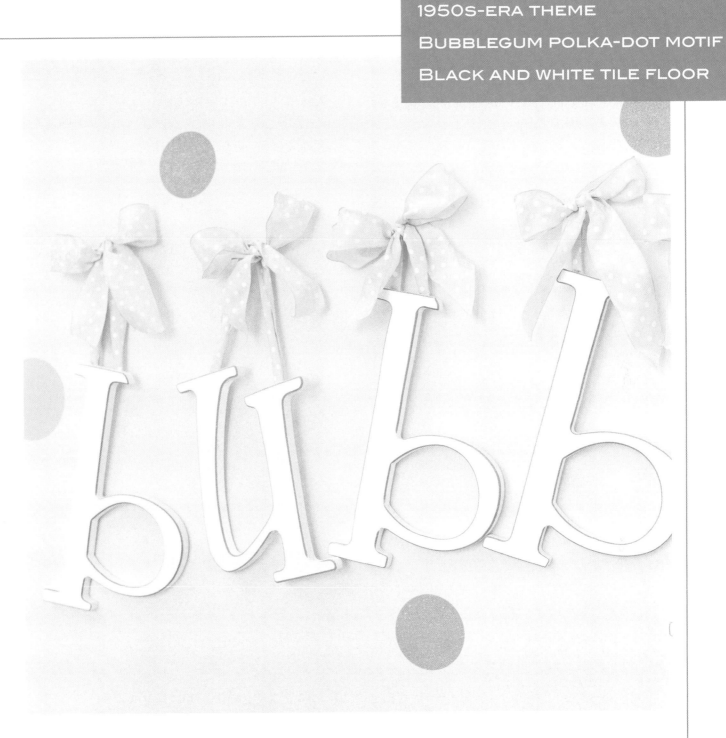

A MOUNTED SHELF FOR TOYS AND ART IS AN OPPORTUNITY TO BOLSTER THE FUN IN THIS BATHROOM.

A SIMPLE PALETTE OF BUBBLEGUM PINK, BLACK, AND WHITE SUMS UP THE 1950S IN A SWEET CANDY WAY.

REFERENCING THE POODLE SKIRTS AND SADDLE SHOES OF A PAST ERA, DECORATIVE DETAILS SET THE MOOD IN THIS BATHROOM.

WOODEN LETTERS HUNG BY RIBBON BOWS SPELL OUT THIS DESIGN'S BUBBLY THEME.

It's Easy Being Green

This spunky kids' bath proves that not only is it easy being green, it's fun as well. A sense of humor and soothing shades of green turn this bathroom into a child's personal pond. There, amiable amphibians (in the form of toys, a soap dispenser, and a washcloth) join him for a splash in the bath.

Large frogs occupy lily pads on the shower curtain, while several smaller fellows serve as curtain hooks above. Joining the frogs, a turtle rug appears to glide across the floor to meet children's wet feet.

The green scheme delivers serene, inviting tones kept lively with vertical-stripe designs on the wall and shower curtain. Touches of blue add visual weight, while a classic white claw-foot tub brings a refined touch to the youthful space. Combining style and wit, these frogs may not become Prince Charming, but they do deliver a touch of enchantment.

A FRIENDLY FROG HANGS AROUND, IMBUING THE ROOM'S DESIGN WITH HUMOR.

A PLUSH TURTLE RUG OFFERS PRACTICAL COMFORT FOR BARE FEET AFTER BATHTIME.

SURE TO BE A CHILD'S FAVORITE DETAIL, FROGS ON LILY PADS SERVE AS HOOKS FOR THE SHOWER CURTAIN.

FUN FROGS—AND OTHER AMPHIBIANS—POP UP BETWEEN VERTICAL GREEN STRIPES IN THIS ENCHANTING CHILDREN'S BATH.

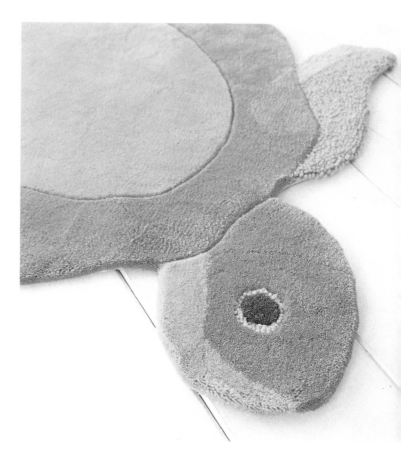

5 KIDS' CORNER

Custom-made spaces for kids are all about fun and activity. Child-size furniture, dress-up clothes, and bright colors are the rule. Beyond that, there are no more rules. Here you'll find not only the familiar playroom but ideas for a slew of cool kid-friendly spots designed to accommodate specific activities. Crafts rooms offer ample space for tackling art projects, teen rooms set the scene for lounging and hip decor, and outdoor playhouses encourage make-believe and independence. These rooms are so clever, even parents want to spend time in them.

COTTAGE IN THE GARAGE

Fantasies of backyard playhouses or forts perched among the branches of a sturdy tree fade when children enter this charming cottage play space located in Beverly and Ray Berry's garage.

The idea for the room came about when, as the couple remodeled their home, Beverly realized there wasn't a spot left for her granddaughters to play. She convinced Ray to transform half of their old garage into a cottage custom-made for dress up and playing house, and Lady Bug Cottage was born.

A tri-fold wall of hinged-together plywood panels divides the playroom from the rest of the garage. One side of the wall is painted to resemble the exterior of a home, complete with a working door. The interior walls, along with the interior of the garage door, are painted to look like the inside of a house including windows and artwork.

Some of the furniture is faux painted on the walls, yet the cottage also includes child-size versions of a refrigerator,

ONE SIDE OF THE TRI-FOLD WALL IS PAINTED TO RESEMBLE THE EXTERIOR OF A HOME. THE WINDOWS, TOPIARIES, AND BRICK STOOP ARE PAINTED ON, BUT THE DOOR IS REAL.

THE TRI-FOLD WALL SEPARATES THE PLAY AREA FROM THE REST OF THE GARAGE. IN THE SUMMER, THE CHILDREN OPEN THE GARAGE DOOR SO THEY CAN PLAY OUTSIDE TOO.

LadyBug COTTAGE

MAIL

sink and stove, table and chairs, and high chairs. Trunks outside of the cottage store dress-up clothing, and Beverly made certain to include an extra-wide mirror so the girls can admire their attire while playing.

"They've accumulated quite a big household," Beverly says. "They vacuum it and clean it and live in it—literally. It's so cute."

Thoughtful planning ensures the space is accessible year-round. During the summer, the garage door opens so the kids can move between the cottage and the driveway to "run errands." A space heater keeps the cottage warm in colder months. Should the need arise, the tri-fold wall and furniture are easy to move to allow a car to park in the garage. That has yet to happen, however, because Lady Bug Cottage is so frequently occupied.

"That little place has been used over and over again by our grandchildren and their little friends as well," Beverly says. "We love to see people's faces when they go in it for the first time—they just break out in this huge smile of delight at seeing the world of make-believe and play."

A WHITE-PAINTED WOODEN REFRIGERATOR AND DINING SET ENSURE HOURS OF FUN PLAYING HOUSE.

THE KITCHEN AREA INCLUDES A SINK, STOVE, AND CABINET STORAGE. SHELVES PAINTED ON THE WALL ABOVE "DISPLAY" DISHWARE AND DECORATIONS.

Backyard Fantasy

A storybook backyard fit for two princesses is just what Lawrie Jordan ordered for his two daughters, Kelly Alaina and Laura. And after the girls leave their playhouse—complete with bunks, TV, phone, computer, and DVD player—the surrounding grounds serve as a quiet place for Lawrie to entertain friends.

Planning the landscape became a project that involved many nightly family discussions about what kind of fish to put in the pond and what design to use for the playhouse. Lawrie called in a team of landscape architects to create a landscape design and to build ponds and waterfalls. He chose the surrounding greenery and water fixtures to complement the existing 80-year-old hardwood trees.

Now the charming playhouse outfitted with all the comforts of home beckons the girls. When they're not in the house, Kelly Alaina and Laura spend time perched on a bench or chair in one of the many seating areas nestled among the foliage.

The garden has become something for everyone in the Jordan family—a play haven for the girls and a quiet oasis for their father.

A CURVING BRIDGE LEADS OVER A STREAM TO THE NEW PLAYHOUSE.

SURROUNDED BY LUSH FOLIAGE, POTTED PLANTS, AND A POND, THE PLAYHOUSE SEEMS FAR AWAY FROM CITY LIFE.

THE PLAYHOUSE NESTLED AMONG THE TREES LOOKS LIKE A MINIATURE VERSION OF A REAL HOME COMPLETE WITH SHINGLES, SHUTTERS, AND LIGHTING TO WELCOME GUESTS.

AUTHENTIC EXTERIOR DETAILS

LANDSCAPING PRESERVES OLD HARDWOODS

INTERIOR AMENITIES OF A REAL HOME

Mini Me

Except for its more diminutive size, the playhouse in Mark and Tami Becker's backyard looks a lot like their real house. Both feature 1915 Craftsman details such as cedar shake shingle siding, period white windows, rock walls, and colorful landscaping.

The loft-style playhouse caters to the Becker's four children. It began as a simple platform but soon evolved into a mini version of the main house. "Once the kids and I started it, I realized it was something we were going to see every day," Mark says. "So we added a roof, ordered windows, and shingled it."

Now the idyllic retreat includes five bunk areas for sleepovers, along with electricity, a TV, and a VCR. When entertaining, the Beckers often feed the kids, then send

them off to the playhouse with a video while grown-ups enjoy a quiet dinner. The playhouse occasionally hosts other guests as well. "Sometimes I sneak out there and take a nap," Mark says.

THE KIDS DECORATED THE WALLS THEMSELVES. PERIOD DETAILS SUCH AS THE BEADED-BOARD PANELING THAT FLANKS BOTTOM BUNKS ECHOES THAT FOUND IN THE MAIN HOUSE.

FROM THE CEDAR SHAKE SHINGLE SIDING TO ROCK WALL SURROUNDING, THIS BACKYARD PLAYHOUSE MIMICS THE LOOK OF THE FAMILY'S CALIFORNIA BUNGALOW.

Nautical Know-How

This nautical-theme play space awash in red, white, and blue ensures that even when bad weather cancels trips to the beach, the kids are never far from ocean fun.

As a theme-appropriate focal point, the homeowners painted a giant compass on the wood floor. The design came from an antique nautical studies book and navigates the perfect positioning of a play table that's really a recycled wooden spool wrapped in nautical white rope. On every open surface, from windowsills to bookshelf to antique end table, model ships sail the high seas. An old American flag, blue-and-white stripe curtains, a set of oars, and fishing gear inspire the imagination to set sail in daily adventures.

A NAUTICAL THEME IS A NATURAL IN THIS SEASIDE HOUSE. A COMPASS PAINTED ON THE FLOOR, MODEL SHIPS DISPLAYED ON SHELVES, AND A SET OF OLD OARS PROPPED IN THE CORNER ARE JUST A FEW OF THE OCEAN-INSPIRED DETAILS.

THE FISHING CORNER INCLUDES A STAINED MAHOGANY TOY TRUNK DECORATED WITH COMPASSES. A LOCALLY CRAFTED TROUT PLAQUE HANGS ABOVE AN ANTIQUE FRENCH HAT RACK THAT HOLDS KIDS' GEAR.

PINT-SIZE COTTAGE

Bunk beds nestled into a miniature home turn a little girl's sleeping area into her own country cottage. Exterior siding, scalloped shakes, fretwork, and plantation shutters build a charming reality. Petite window boxes and porch railings constructed from common lumber make the little cottage even more genuine.

The front porch greets guests with pots of flowers and a doorbell that plays 30 different tunes. The door is made from wood trim attached to plywood and finished off with a brass-plated drawer pull used as a miniature doorknob. The bedroom's outside wall serves as the fourth wall of the cottage; the window there brightens both bunks.

The lower platform bed rests right inside the front entrance. To access the upper bunk, guests must walk around to the side of the home and ascend a short flight of stairs. Decorative tulips lead the way. An opening in the roofline allows children to peek down to the activity below.

A HANDRAIL MAKES THE CLIMB TO THE UPPER BUNK SAFER. THE ARCHITECTURAL DETAILS ON A LITTLE DOGHOUSE MIMIC THE PLAYHOUSE'S FACADE.

WORKING LIGHTS INSIDE AND OUTSIDE THE PLAYHOUSE LEND GENUINE CHARM AND ACT AS NIGHT-LIGHTS.

SILK FLOWER VINES CLIMB THE PORCH RAILING AND BRIGHTEN WINDOW BOXES AND PLANTERS.

Teen Sweet

Transforming an empty attic awash in white into a hip teen suite requires little more than the right combination of texture and color. Who would ever guess that this space—decked out with clean-lined furnishings and colorful accessories—occupies the attic of a 1900s Victorian-style home?

The under-the-eve suite posed many challenges, including short walls and sloped ceilings. Designer Jeni Hilpipre-Wright dealt with the room's shortcomings by keeping the walls and ceiling white, calling on accessories to banish blandness, and using rugs to dictate divisions within the suite.

Every furnishing is as hardworking as it is good-looking. Pieces sit low to the ground, making angled walls seem higher and creating an uninterrupted visual plane. In the sitting area, the magenta sofas form a sectional or separate to expand sleeping space. Inexpensive modular cubes play off the room's angled ceiling in a stair-step fashion. They also hold a juicy assemblage of vases, bowls, and plates. The clean lines of the ceiling fixtures and glass tables are unobtrusive, allowing the colorful elements to take center stage.

Rugs delineate the separation between living spaces. In the sitting area, a fuzzy white rug pairs with the glass table. A smaller, bolder pointillistic rug designates a study zone in the transition space between the sitting area and bedroom. A modern desk and orange chair provide the perfect spot for catching up on homework. In the nearby bedroom, an orange area rug over the carpet makes a clear transition from sitting to sleeping areas.

Although the white walls are mostly unadorned, the exposed brick, angled ceilings, and decorative elements ensure an interesting vibe. The wall art consists of narrow framed prints that lean against the wall on a ledge near the desk area. Nearby, a piece of abstract art is propped on a dresser. Sections of exposed brick that flank the entry to the bedroom allude to the home's original architecture.

The accessories in this suite play an important role. From pottery to wall-hung pajamas to pillows, eye candy provides unity through the consistent use of color. "When you take all this stuff out, it's just a plain-Jane vanilla space," Wright says.

EVEN THE SOFA SECTIONAL IN THE LIVING SPACE IS VISUALLY LIGHT THANKS TO ITS MODERN-MINDED STYLE AND PLAYFUL HUE. SUMPTUOUS VELVET UPHOLSTERY IS PURE BLISS FOR LOUNGING.

Furniture sitting low to the ground

Rugs to delineate living spaces

Colorful details with white walls

ARTWORK PROPPED ON A DRESSER LENDS A CASUAL ABSTRACT ELEMENT.

WHEN PAJAMAS ARE AS SWANKY AS THIS STRIPED SET, WHY NOT HANG THEM AS ART?

WHITE WALLS, A LARGE OVERHEAD LAMP, AND CUSHY WHITE RUG KEEP THE SPACE BRIGHT DESPITE THE TINY WINDOW.

In the sitting area, translucent modular cubes visually recede into the wall, making accessories seem like they're floating.

Shapely accessories like those on the coffee table bring this suite to life.

CLUTTER BEGONE

Ask any parent and they're sure to tell you: Kids come with a lot of stuff. From diapers and rattles to trucks and dolls, children's accoutrements can fill a home and leave room for little else. Julie and Michael Tracy decided to get their kids' clutter under control and to provide a special place for play at the same time. With a second-story addition over their garage and family room, they built a space chock-full of nooks and crannies—suited to both toddler and teen.

The couple turned to architects Fred Wilson and Bob Zuber, whose design works its way around a flue that rises

THE SUNNY ROOM IS PERFECTLY SET UP FOR KIDS— AND MOM—TO PLAY. THE WINDOWS HARMONIZE WITH THOSE IN THE REST OF THE HOUSE.

CRAYONS, MARKERS, BASKETS, AND BOOKS ALL FIND A PLACE ON EXPANSIVE OPEN SHELVES.

WICKER BASKETS PROVE THAT STORAGE OPTIONS
SOMETIMES MAKE GREAT DESIGN ELEMENTS. THESE
EVEN MATCH THE SEATS OF THE CHAIRS.

from the fireplace in a downstairs family room. Their unique solution encases the flue while adding more storage. Two narrow closets, which leave room for shelving nooks, form a hallway that leads to a balcony. The closets store bulky items such as blankets and seasonal decorations in bins, while the open shelving units on either side of the closets are filled with baskets and clear containers. The solution also acts as a natural divider, breaking the space into a play area, office room for mom, and a gathering spot. "Those little shelves were a stroke of genius," Julie says.

The ambience is light and cheery, thanks to a glass-pane door and generous double-hung windows that match those in the rest of the house. A spacious rag rug softens the hardwood in the central play space. Magnetic and tack boards enable children to see what's on the daily schedule and to display photos and much-loved mementos.

A white built-in storage unit faces the windows, with open shelves on the top half and cabinets to enclose messier items on the bottom.

When all that kid stuff has a place, it's not such a bad thing after all.

A CLOSET MASKS A FIREPLACE FLUE RISING FROM THE FAMILY ROOM BELOW. THE SHORT HALLWAY LEADS TO A BALCONY.

THE OPEN LAYOUT LENDS ITSELF TO PLAYTIME. A WEALTH OF EASILY ACCESSIBLE STORAGE SPACE MEANS KIDS CAN PICK UP AFTER THEMSELVES.

CREATIVE CONTROL

THE MULTICOLOR TILE ESTABLISHES A PLAYFUL SETTING, WHILE HANDY BINS AND CONTAINERS ENCOURAGE EFFICIENT ACTIVITY.

WITH A SETUP LIKE THIS, THE KIDS' CREATIVITY AND IMAGINATIONS ARE FREE TO SOAR—AND THEY WON'T MESS UP THE HOUSE WHILE THEY'RE AT IT.

Children's creativity and messes go hand in hand. Crafts and projects may keep the imagination active, but they can be hard on a home's orderly appearance. Rather than trying to fit her children's activities into the rest of her home, Karen Siegal decided to build a room that would fit their activities.

"My theory on kids and creativity," she says, "is that they will only use what is easily accessible to them and organized in a way they can work with."

The home now boasts a designated craft room where the Siegal daughters may create and build without distraction or inconvenience. A central island welcomes artists with a broad work space and plenty of storage in undercounter drawers. Topped with dark slate, the island provides a desklike area that is easily cleaned and can function as a chalkboard. The walls' white tongue-and-groove siding and natural light from a nearby window establish an attractive, vibrant space for the children. A blue ceiling sets a soothing tone, while accents in solid colors encourage a playful, imaginative atmosphere.

The room's tone draws the children in, and the island and hutch provide handy organization that helps them stay on task. Glass cabinet doors keep supplies in view, making selection quick and order uncomplicated. The hutch's long line of cabinets and drawers delivers plenty of storage and conceals large bins of materials. Frequently used supplies remain at hand along the green tiled countertop. "Kids aren't going to get into painting if they can't find the paint," Karen explains. A computer desk tucked in the corner gives Karen a space to work as well.

School assignments and rainy-day projects are more than welcome at the Siegal household now that it has a space dedicated to personal expression. With a room of their own, the children may engage in creative activity knowing they are free to explore and imagine. "Since I'm very big on keeping things neat and on making things instead of buying them, a craft room fills many needs for us," Karen says. "If it's a mess, we can just close the door and cut it off from the rest of the house."

COLORFUL EASY-TO-CLEAN TILE

GLASS CABINET DOORS FOR VIEWS OF SUPPLIES

SLATE FOR A DURABLE WORK SURFACE

A BUILT-IN DESK ECHOES THE HUTCH'S COLORFUL DESIGN AND PROVIDES SPACE FOR MOM TO WORK WHILE THE KIDS CREATE.

A ROOM DEDICATED TO CRAFT PROJECTS KEEPS COLORFUL CREATIVE CHAOS SEPARATE FROM THE LIVING SPACES JUST OUTSIDE THE DOORS.

Homework Haven

Homework is less of a hassle and easier to tackle in this clever space for five schoolchildren and their parents. Without a central spot for projects, the family and their clutter scattered throughout the house. Now everyone gathers in one room to work on individual assignments as well as family projects.

An expanse of desk space along the exterior walls is perfect for cracking the books, while a central table provides plenty of elbow room for art or science projects. A large single-basin sink helps contain messes. "Crafting and cleanup make water necessary," designer Louise Brooks says, "and with a sink right here, no one needs to traipse through the halls carrying water."

A peaked roof and plenty of windows lend a spacious, airy feel. Traditional cabinetry and dark wood floors and furnishings mimic elements found in the rest of the home and add a touch of formality.

"Don't let it fool you," Brooks says. "Every surface in this place is durable, easy-to-clean, and can stand up to paint and glue."

The space can easily evolve into a studio or home office once the children are out of the house.

THIS 20×20-FOOT ADDITION ABOVE THE KITCHEN HARBORS MULTIPLE WORKSTATIONS AND AMPLE STORAGE FOR HOMEWORK, CRAFTS, AND OTHER PROJECTS.

A LARGE SINK MAKES CLEANUP SIMPLE. THE WRAPPING STATION CAN ALSO STORE REAMS OF ART PAPER.

BASKETS FOR STASHING CRAFTING SUPPLIES

BUILT-IN SINK FOR EASY CLEANUP

CENTRAL TABLE FOR STUDYING AND LARGE PROJECTS

FRUITFUL FUSION

Suspended between the charm of childhood and the maturity of adulthood, a young adult needs a space that accommodates increasing independence and reflects the vitality of a changing life. According to designer Traci Baldus, an apartment-style teen suite meets the necessary requirements. She rigged this one with an explosion of vibrant color, plus rooms and spaces outfitted for specific activities.

Vivid colors establish a suitably audacious attitude in the lively bedroom suite. Lime-and-white-striped wallpaper creates an active visual space, while the soothing green tone maintains a soft atmosphere. White carpet provides a clean foundation for a shag rug, two ottomans, and the bedcovers, all in bright orange and shocking pink. Check patterns on pillows, sheets, and rugs perpetuate the energetic, visual feast.

Countering the bright color scheme is a crisp contemporary style. A vanity beside the entry to the bedroom provides a place for dressing and starting the day, as well as plenty of room for clothes, makeup, and other storage needs. Connecting the two drawer towers of the vanity, a wood countertop partners with a wall-mounted mirror. A grouping of rectangular boxes suspended on the opposite wall echo the check fabric patterns while repeating the vanity's more mature wood presence. The varied shelf shapes provide storage and display spaces for books, CDs, pictures, and more.

A green-and-white stripe chaise lounge in yet another corner of the room matches the striped wallpaper. The bright orange shag rug establishes the area as another distinct space. Light from the adjacent window, an end table made to hold books and magazines, and the comfortable throw pillows make it a kick-back retreat for reading or relaxing.

GREEN STRIPED WALLPAPER SETS THIS BEDROOM'S COLORFUL TONE, WHILE A CONTEMPORARY BED FRAME AND WOODEN SHELVES OFFER STYLISTIC FLEXIBILITY.

Brilliant hues and active patterns bind the bedroom to a connected sitting room, ideal for hanging out with friends or banking time alone. Its solid green walls, orange chairs, and check ottoman borrow from the bedroom, but never copy. Attached to the ceiling, curtain cables support a sheer white check fabric in front of a green panel to deliver a soft, breezy frame for the room's broad window bank.

The room's occupant can explore her creativity in the artist's studio, a separate part of the sitting room. The drafting table accommodates the creation of masterpieces … or homework. When she needs a break, the teen can pause from her work and gaze out the window for inspiration.

An artist's table suits the design's creative character and doubles as a quiet retreat for homework.

Green walls and orange chairs in the lounge area echo the bedroom's palette and patterns, establishing a unified sensibility.

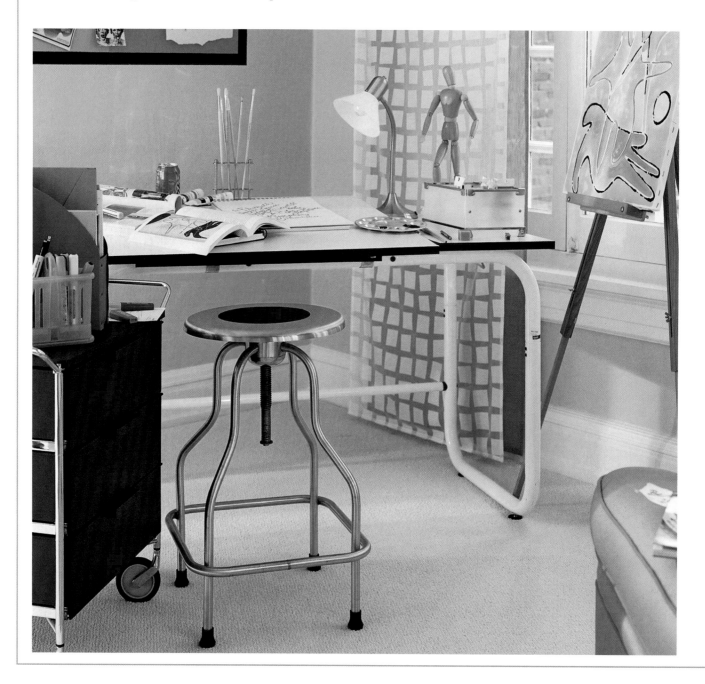

Sleek modern maple drawers and a matching countertop deliver a vanity that promises to work in future decorating schemes.

A vibrant combination of colors and patterns promotes a youthful vitality in the sitting area.

WORK AND PLAY

A Swedish country-inspired two-room suite is much more than a bedroom for Christina Dorobeck. Her versatile living space also boasts an organized study room and a comfy gathering place for friends.

Working with interior designer Catherine Bailly Dunne, Christina requested a sitting area where she could catch a movie or chill with friends. A multipurpose daybed serves as both a cozy perch for TV viewing and an extra bed for impromptu sleepovers. Two swiveling chenille-covered armchairs entice friends to sink in with a bowl of popcorn. The television is housed in a whitewashed armoire.

While the sleeping and sitting area provides a place to schmooze and snooze, an adjacent room finds new life as a work space. Here Christina does her homework and tackles school projects with friends. Fresh greens and purples radiate the room's Swedish style and work well with new whitewashed furniture. The classic pieces can grow along with Christina and eventually move to her first apartment or remain as the furniture for a guest room.

Christina and her mother, Julie, found a vintage walnut desk at a California antique shop when Christina was 12. "I loved the curvy top and the fact that it had drawers for everything," Christina says. When it came time to redo the room, keeping the piece was a must. Dunne had it stripped and stained to match the new furnishings. It now serves the more mature role of vanity. Christina decorated the wall around the mirror with photos from fashion magazines.

The study area includes a roomy table and chairs where Christina and friends play cards or dive into class projects. "Having two distinct rooms in the suite helps separate study time and hang-out time," Dunne says. "It makes homework more focused and relaxing more fun."

LUSH GREENS AND PURPLES HARMONIZE WITH THE CLEAN, WHITEWASHED FURNITURE.

A SWEDISH-STYLE DAYBED SERVES AS A SOFA AND EXTRA BED WHEN FRIENDS VISIT. IT ALSO PROVIDES A PLACE FOR CHRISTINA TO RELAX AND WORK ON HOMEWORK.

SEPARATE SITTING AND STUDY AREAS
TELEVISION HIDDEN IN A WHITEWASHED ARMOIRE
DAYBED AS COUCH AND EXTRA SLEEPING SPOT

Overstuffed swiveling chairs and a television hidden in the armoire turn the sitting room into a home theater.

Christina and friends can discuss class projects at the roomy table and chairs, then step out to a small porch for fresh air.

A WALL OF BUILT-IN SHELVES AND CABINETS ENDS
WITH A BUILT-IN DESK.

ALL ABOUT ART

Two mobiles reminiscent of sculptor Alexander Calder's work inspired designer Shelly Handman and painter Lidia Wylangowska to apply their artistic appreciation to this Chicago-area playroom.

Using bright purple, red, green, and gold, Wylangowska painted the room in both geometric designs and solid colors that bring to mind the work of artist Piet Mondrian. She gave a plain window a stained-glass effect with artist's oils and spray paint and used picture molding to make a faux window through which two art thief characters, Gus and Lucky, peer into the room.

Handman says practicality and function come before aesthetics when planning a playroom, but that doesn't mean they have to be bland. The playroom "has a level of sophistication [that makes it] art," Handman says.

The kids use this basement for all kinds of play, including painting, drawing, and sculpting with clay. And even though it's meant for the kids, Handman says, "adults enjoy being down there too."

TWO MOBILES PLANTED THE SEEDS FOR AN ARTISTIC BACKDROP OF BOLD SHAPES AND BRIGHT COLORS.

TWO OF ARTIST LIDIA WYLANGOWSKA'S HANDPAINTED CHARACTERS, ART THIEVES GUS AND LUCKY, PEER FROM A PICTURE MOLDING MADE TO LOOK LIKE A WINDOW. THE LEDGE DISGUISES HOUSE MECHANICS UNDERNEATH.

Home Room

School days represent some of the most treasured memories of childhood. With its chalkboard, desks, and bulletin boards, the classroom introduces children to best friends, beloved books, and a world of learning. Rather than relegating the charm of classroom style to the schoolhouse, this clever kids' room brings the school spirit home, blending fun and learning in one playful space.

Vintage style and schoolhouse accessories coordinate to build this room's nostalgic feel. A pastel yellow table sits at the head of the class, offering project space in the shape of a teacher's desk. A wardrobe-like cabinet echoes the desk's sophisticated style, and a nearby set of small lockers provides traditional storage. Sleek and refinished, a standard child's desk shares a corner with cushy kids' armchairs.

Beaded-board wainscoting promotes a nostalgic air, and the walls evoke a distinctive classroom sensibility. Reminiscent of a schoolroom blackboard, a long strip of chalkboard paint forms a border above the wainscoting, allowing children to practice their writing or exercise their imaginations on the walls. A tree mural sets the mood in an attractive reading nook, and its magnetic paint encourages children to experiment with letters printed on metal leaves. A school bus message board with magnetic strip stripes and bulletin board windows serves as a handy space for keepsakes and photos of friends.

The design intermingles learning and fun but also remains a comfortable retreat for quiet relaxation or an active play date. A thick multicolor area rug provides ready-made

This clever school bus displays favorite items using pushpins and magnets.

Pennants hung from the curtain rod establish an old school spirit.

Warm colors and soft chairs combine with classic schoolroom features for a fun and engaging play space.

Chalkboard paint border
Magnetic tree mural
Hopscotch rug

space for board games and creative projects. Capturing the mood of recess in an indoor space, a hopscotch rug invites children to play at any hour, in any weather.

The result: A clever room that brings the fun parts of school home.

A HOPSCOTCH RUG ENCOURAGES RECESS AT ALL HOURS OF THE DAY.

THE TREE OF KNOWLEDGE SHADES THE READING CORNER. A RAG RUG AND COMFY CHAIRS INSPIRE SPRAWLING.

SUGGESTING A TEACHER'S DESK AT THE HEAD OF THE CLASS, A PASTEL VINTAGE-STYLE TABLE OFFERS SPACE FOR SMALL PROJECTS.

PLENTY OF PLAY

The decor may suggest rain clouds and stormy skies, but this kids' playroom has anything but a dark and dreary outlook. Designer Jodi Mensing used simple, inexpensive techniques to create a perfect sun-showery retreat.

First Mensing divided the room into nooks of multiple entertainment spaces using colors drawn from the great outdoors—white, blue, and green—and clever placement of furniture and accessories. Two shades of fair-weather blue cover the ceiling and the walls, clouds of white latex paint mixed with a touch of blue drift along on the ceiling, and green accessories complete the outdoor-inspired scheme.

A scaled-down easel for little painters displays works in progress. A lime green table and four stools provide a

RUBBER RAIN BOOTS ATTACHED TO THE WALL WITH HOOKS OR SCREWS STASH SUPPLIES AT KID HEIGHT.

CLOUDS FLOAT OVERHEAD, AND YELLOW DAISIES POP FROM THE ARTIFICIAL-TURF CARPET BELOW. FLOWER PETALS ALSO BLOOM ON THE STOOLS' SEATS.

work surface for kids and playmates, and its easy-care top makes cleanup a snap. Mensing carried the outdoor theme to the stools' flower cushions, using bright yellow fabric for the centers and red for layers of petals sewn along the edges. Under the table and stool set, a remnant piece of artificial grass edged with bright yellow rickrack serves as carpet. Sewn-on plastic daisies seemingly grow from the ground beneath. Rubber rain boots, hung from the wall with either screws or hooks, corral art supplies such as washable paints and markers.

While the easel and table encourage creative expression, other accents in the room stimulate interest in geography and science. A wall-hung interactive weather report and vinyl stick-on letters, symbols, and numbers allow future forecasters to predict the week's weather. Two armchairs covered in light green polka-dot fabric that matches the color of the window treatments beckon children, inspiring them to read or watch a movie with friends.

Function and budget dictated many of the room's pieces. A matching dresser and armoire add inexpensive storage space for toys, books, and games. On the armoire, a short curtain held with a tension rod conceals often-used items. Mini storage bins in bright rainbow hues allow kids to find glue, scissors, and crayons, and enable adults to easily note any supplies in need of replenishment. Self-adhesive scrapbooking page pebbles denote the contents of each container.

Strands of clear glass beads rain from the spokes of a suspended umbrella.

Pint-size Picassos can use the easel to whip up new creations or display finished ones.

Fleece and fuzzy wool make warm, fluffy cloud pillows.

The sun-shower theme lends itself to clever accenting. A pint-size ceiling-hung plastic umbrella shields those below from the pelting "rain"—actually strands of clear glass beads attached to the spokes. A doll's raincoat tops a polka-dot lampshade, and sunshine finials cap the curtain rods.

If wind, rain, or snow keeps your little ones inside, there's enough magic in the weather—and in a playroom designed for indoor fun—to while away any weather-dreary day. And as an added bonus, you'll never have to look far for slickers or galoshes.

Index